KID G~~~~~~~~AL

AN INSIDER'S GUIDE TO
GROWN-UPS

# KID CONFIDENTIAL
## AN INSIDER'S GUIDE TO GROWN-UPS

## Monte Montgomery

illustrated by Patricia Storms

Walker & Company ✺ New York

First published in the United States of America in March 2012
by Walker Publishing Company, Inc., a division of Bloomsbury Publishing, Inc.
www.bloomsburykids.com

For information about permission to reproduce selections from this book, write to
Permissions, Walker BFYR, 175 Fifth Avenue, New York, New York 10010

Library of Congress Cataloging-in-Publication Data
Montgomery, Monte.
Kid confidential: an insider's guide to grown-ups / Monte Montgomery ;
illustrated by Patricia Storms.
p.     cm.
ISBN 978-0-8027-8643-2 (hardcover)  •  ISBN 978-0-8027-2353-6 (paperback)
1. Children — Juvenile humor. 2. Adulthood — Juvenile humor. 3. Wit and humor, Juvenile.
I. Storms, Patricia. II. Title.
PN6231.C32M66 2011          818'.602 — dc22          2011010942

Typeset in Alphabet Soup, Bruno JB Std, Andy Std, Vanquish, and Didot
Book design by Yelena Safronova

Printed in the U.S.A. by Quad/Graphics, Fairfield, Pennsylvania
1  3  5  7  9  10  8  6  4  2  (hardcover)
1  3  5  7  9  10  8  6  4  2  (paperback)

For Clavo, my partner in all things —M. M.

For my Guido, who assures me that he will never
become a grown-up —P. S.

# TABLE OF CONTENTS

## Part 4: Grown-Ups in the Wild

# PREFACE

You've seen them.

*Big, tall, odd-looking creatures driving cars, ordering expensive meals in restaurants, using bizarre words that only they seem to understand, and generally strutting around as if they own the place—which, unfortunately, they do.*

*Let's face it: adults aren't going to let you have the world until you pry it out of their cold, dead hands. But that doesn't leave you helpless against them. If you really want to drive grown-ups crazy . . . observe them. Figure out what makes them tick. Understand them. It'll blow their minds—and yours.*

*The fact is, you owe it to yourself to learn everything you can about grown-ups. That's because (a.) you're stuck with them for the time being, and (b.) no matter how you feel about it, one day (sooner than you think!) you'll become one. Revolting? Not necessarily. You don't have to end up like them. The only person who decides what kind of grown-up you are when you grow up is . . . you.*

# A Grammatical Note

Throughout this book you may spot the words "they," "them," and "their" in places where a strict grammarian would insist on "he," "him," "his," "he or she," "him or her," or "his or her"—as in:

*If some language snob objects to the use of the word "they," let them write their own darned book.*

Although this usage is, strictly speaking, "wrong," the author figures that (a.) using the default pronouns "he," "him," and "his" to refer to a population that is slightly more than half female is *more* wrong, and (b.) cluttering up the book with a bunch of clumsy "his and hers"-es is even more wronger yet.

As a lifelong maniac for correct grammar, spelling, and punctuation, the author found this adjustment extremely painful to make, but him will get over it.

# Admit It: Childhood Stinks!

Most grown-ups forget how crummy their childhoods were. By age twenty-one or so, a sort of "post-traumatic-childhood amnesia" sets in, leaving them with misty memories of playground triumphs, slumber parties, and puppy love rather than the much creepier (and accurate) ones of nightmares, skinned knees, and pinkeye. This explains why so many grown-ups go on to have kids of their own and then are baffled when those kids start complaining about something totally minor, like home-work or acne.

When you think about it, why *shouldn't* childhood stink? Compared with older folks, young people are inexperienced, frightened, naive, powerless, and short. They're easily bullied by adults, bigger kids, even the larger household pets. And the ordeal continues for well over a *dozen long years*—which, from a kid's per-spective, feels like about a hundred. (Remember how long third grade dragged on? See chapter 8, "The Rela-tive Nature of Time," to find out why.)

This book is the result of long, painful research into the alien territory of adulthood, where perils and pitfalls lurk around every corner. And just as it would be irresponsible to send clueless travelers to strange cities without a map, or plunge them into jungles without a basic description of some of the danger-ous creatures they're likely to encounter, it would be wrong to turn defenseless children loose in suburban jungles prowled by parents, teachers, doctors, and waiters with bushy mustaches.

## This Book's Mission

The purpose of *Kid Confidential* is twofold:

1. To serve as a useful guide for forward-thinking boys and girls who are hungry for information

about their age-old foe, The Mature Adult (*Humanus Giganticus*)—such as how to identify various types and subtypes, how they got that way, and why they act so ridiculous; and

2. To provide diabolical tactics and strategies that will help level the playing field in the time-honored, age-old struggle between You and Them . . . because They have had the upper hand just about long enough. Each of these tactics will appear in a special box, like the following:

TRICKERY TACTICS

# Tactic #1:
# Duck and Cover!

To avoid being hugged by an extradisgusting adult, drop quickly to one knee and pretend to tie your shoes. Take an incredibly long time to do this. The adult will eventually grow bored and wander off in search of another victim.

*Kid Confidential* will also offer up brief sketches of various "Types of Adults," and will reveal three Universal Truths—good advice no matter how young (or old) you are.

What do you say we get started?

# What Is a Grown-Up?

Loosely defined, a grown-up is anyone who (a.) is a lot older than you, (b.) has stopped growing taller (but may still be growing wider), (c.) reads newspapers, and (d.) thinks the music you listen to is garbage.

But grown-ups have much in common with you as well.

The Big Similarity is that adults never really stop *feeling* like the person they were when they were little. Even when they look in the mirror and see wrinkles (they'll call them "smile lines"), they still feel like the same nine- or ten-year-old who innocently grinned back at them from the mirror allllll those years ago.

This explains why grown-ups will sometimes catch a glimpse of themselves in a photo that somebody took from an unflattering angle, do a shudder take, and exclaim, "Man, am I getting old!"

Other things that never change as people get older are certain likes and dislikes. No matter how old they get, adults still like: sunshine, laughing hard enough to shoot milk out of their nose, the taste of chocolate, the smell of baking bread, the feel of hitting a baseball squarely, and compliments. And they never stop *disliking*: pain, being pushed around, losing a quarter down a drain, not being able to get to sleep, the sound of a cockroach being squashed, and the smell of burning rubber (unless they created it themselves by flooring their new Mercedes at a green light).

There are, of course, many differences as well. We'll be going into these in painful detail. As you read this book, you'll develop a deeper knowledge of the Mysterious Adult—mind, body, and spirit. After all, you're stuck with them for a while (without them, who would drive you to soccer practice?) and the odds are that it's going to be a good long time before you get your final revenge (by outliving them), so you might as well understand them.

**A Pop Quiz**

Before continuing, here's a quick test to determine whether you yourself are a grown-up.

1. Your idea of a good time is:
    (a.) Dangling string cheese from your nose
    (b.) Playing with dolls
    (c.) Comparing health insurance policies

2. Which of the following do you like taking two at a time?
    (a.) Scoops of ice cream
    (b.) Stairs
    (c.) Pills

3. If you met a 29-year-old man, what would you call him?
    (a.) Sir
    (b.) Grandpa
    (c.) Young fella

**4.** Which expression do you use most often?
    (a.) Awesome!
    (b.) Cool!
    (c.) Bah, humbug!

**5.** Your best look is:
    (a.) Bangs
    (b.) Curls
    (c.) Progressive lenses

**6.** Your teeth are:
    (a.) Straight
    (b.) Crooked
    (c.) Next to your bed

**7.** Your favorite kind of party is:
    (a.) Birthday
    (b.) Halloween
    (c.) Republican

Count one point for every (a.) or (b.) and two points for every (c.). If you scored a seven, you're a kid. If you scored anything higher than a seven, you are a *bona fide* adult and *should not be reading this book*. Please give it to the next kid you see. They need it more than you do.

# PART 1:
# ANATOMY OF A
# GROWN-UP

**T**he fully grown human being is one of nature's wonders. Then again, so is the fully grown warthog. The difference is that the warthog will never get after you to clean up your room. This is one of the many reasons that warthogs make excellent pets.

Getting back to grown-ups. To understand their curious ways, we must get inside their skin. Not literally, as this would be very uncomfortable both for you and the adult. But there's no avoiding it—to comprehend the mind, we must start with the body. Ready? Let's get physical!

# 1
## FLESH AND BONES
### Why Adults Can't Keep Their Minds Off Their Bodies

Grown-ups never seem to shut up about their bodies: what goes into them, what comes out of them, and how to dress them up. If you hear a person use the words "biceps," "lactose intolerant," "carbs," "accessorize," "nutrition," "hygiene," "perspiration," or "sale at Nordstrom," it's a safe bet that you've got an adult on your hands.

Kids, in contrast, pretty much take their bodies for granted. To them the whole arms/legs/head/torso arrangement has one major function—to get around in—and a few minor ones, such as sports, tree climbing, beating up smaller kids, and escaping from bigger ones. It would never occur to anyone under the age of, say, fifteen to spend hours reading magazine articles about how to acquire six-pack abs, shop for vitamins, or reduce cholesterol, whatever cholesterol is. But an adult's very *identity* is often based on the appearance and condition of what is really nothing more than machinery.

Adults are obsessed with bodies—theirs and other people's—for several reasons:

- **They're insecure.** Grown-ups are always comparing themselves with other grown-ups to see who looks better. And even though exactly half of them are below average and the other half are above average (this is, in fact, what the word "average" means), 95 percent of adults are convinced that they look worse than the other 5 percent. Advertisers make tons of money off this fear, because adults will buy absolutely anything if they think it'll improve their looks. (Next time you get a chance, check out the old "hair in a can" commercials online. You'll never stop laughing.)

## Tactic #2:
## Handling Insecure Adults

Once in a great while an old person will ask a young person to comment on some specific aspect of the old person's appearance. *Don't do it.* If they persist, there's one safe way out: paste a huge smile on your face and say, "You look great!" It doesn't matter if they really look like something that came out of a clogged sink; grown-ups always love to hear this sentence, even if they don't believe it.

- **They're vain.** Vanity is the flip side of insecurity. When grown-ups think they look good, they think they look *very*, *very* good, which is why they're so *soooooo* into what they wear. And it's true that a nice outfit can disguise a lot of imperfections. Even a chimpanzee looks pretty good in a well-cut business suit (although the sleeves are too short).

## Note to Boys: What's the Deal with Suits?

At some point you're going to find yourself strapped into one of these stiff, starchy straitjackets for a tribal ritual like a wedding or funeral. Feels awful, doesn't it? That's because a suit has only one function: to identify you as a person who wears a suit. Comfort never enters the picture. In fact, the only times you won't notice how tight and awkward they feel is at your *own* wedding (because you'll be so nervous) and your *own* funeral (for obvious reasons).

## Note to Girls: What's the Deal with Heels?

If you're not already wearing heels, you soon will be. Just standing upright on these crazy stilts is an athletic event on the order of the balance beam, and when the job is made even harder by bumpy sidewalks or subway gratings, disaster often follows. Most embarrassing of all is wearing heels to a garden party. If you stand in one spot long enough, you start to melt into the lawn like the Wicked Witch of the West.

⊙ **They're sickos.** As a rule of thumb, the older you get, the worse your health. This is mostly because bodies, like Tickle Me Elmo dolls, simply wear out. But there's an upside to this disease, too: it gives adults something to talk about—namely, medical conditions. It's almost like a contest, only the one with the *worst* disease wins.

## Adult Injuries

**S**ticks and stones may break their bones, but they'll forget all about it the next day. That's right; a surprising benefit of being a grown-up is that pain hurts less.

For a kid, every splinter, every sprain, and every stubbed toe is the focus of intense interest for days. Getting a few stitches can keep a class of second graders buzzing for a week. The question "Did you cry?" becomes hugely important ("I did not!" "You did, too!"), and the debate rages on until someone else tops it with something really exotic, like a tonsillectomy.

Contrast this with an adult. It's not uncommon to see a forty-year-old sporting a scrape or bruise the size of a pot holder without any idea of how they got it (especially if they were out late the night before).

# Tactic #3:
# Silencing the Sick

If you're ever trapped with a gang of geezers yammering on and on about their bursitis, arthritis, or something-else-itis and you can't take it another second, tug on the sleeve of the oldest male in the room and ask him, "What's a prostate?" This will shut them all up, or at least get them off the subject.

# Kid/Grown-Up Comparison Chart
## You vs. Them, from Top to Bottom

### Male Version:

**Hair:** Migrates to where it's not wanted (chest, back, knuckles).

**Hair:** Stays where it's wanted (head).

**Ears:** Sensitive to very quiet sounds such as you talking on the phone after lights out, three rooms away.

**Ears:** Sensitive to nonexistent sounds, such as vampires sharpening their fangs under the bed.

**Teeth:** High-maintenance—addiction to bleaching, veneers, and brightening, whitening tartar-reducing toothpaste can result in a smile that looks like a row of washing machines.

**Teeth:** Low-maintenance—just brush and floss regularly.

**Legs:** Weak, sore, creaky; unable to run long distances, unless they're chasing you.

**Legs:** Sturdy, able to run long distances.

**Toenails:** Thicken with age; saws or bolt-cutters sometimes required.

**Toenails:** No problem.

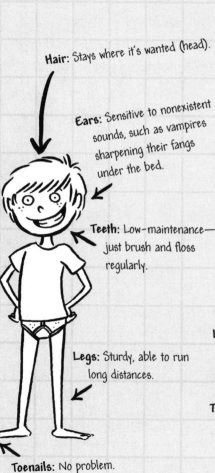

# Female Version:

**Hair:** Always too long or too short or too straight or too curly or too thick or too thin or the wrong color or (even worse) lacking "luster." An industry the size of Microsoft has grown to deal with these challenges.

**Hair:** Wash it, dry it, forget it.

**Ears:** Able to withstand even the loudest sounds, such as earbuds cranked up to 11.

**Ears:** Deaf to unwanted sounds, such as your requests for cash.

**Nails:** Ultrahigh-maintenance—manicures, polishes, acrylics, resins, extensions, press-ons, and wraps that cost enough to feed a family of five.

**Nails:** Low-maintenance—easily filed or chewed to proper length.

**Butt:** Convenient to sit on.

**Butt:** Constant source of worry, as in, "Does my butt look fat in this skirt/dress/pantsuit/light/restaurant/century?"

**Feet:** Fine with most shoes, the more comfortable the better.

**Feet:** Owns fifty pairs of shoes, and they all hurt.

# 2
# FEEDING TIME
## Are They Really Going to Eat That?

You know what you like: burgers, pizza, chicken fingers, and ice cream. But the older people get, the more they gravitate toward stuff that's weird-looking, odd-smelling, or just plain gross—especially if it's expensive, rare, or has a fancy name like "pâté de foie gras" (goose-liver paste) or "pousse-café" (multilayered cocktail). Here's why:

○ **Food.** We all remember our first whiff of Parmesan cheese. Some kids like it right off the bat (they're called "Italians"). To the rest of us, it smelled like vomit. But a strange thing happens along the road to adulthood. One day somebody sprinkles it on a slice of pizza while you're not looking, and you take a bite and it's kind of sharp and interesting, and later you do some sprinkling yourself, and eventually pasta tastes bland and boring without it, and the next thing you know you've become a Parmesaniac.

   Parmesan is known as a "gateway cheese" because it leads directly to the hard stuff:

Camembert, bleu, and Gorgonzola. (But not to Limburger. Nobody ever gets used to Limburger.)

## Tactic #4:
## Dietary Defenses

Even larger than the difference between what adults like now and what they liked as kids is the difference between what *they* eat (like lobster) and what they make *you* eat (like broccoli). They defend this inconsistency with the most devastating weapon in the entire grown-up arsenal: "Do as I say, not as I do." Unfortunately, the only way to fight this is by growing up, moving out, becoming an excellent cook, and throwing great dinner parties—but not inviting your parents.

- **Coffee.** As people age, the natural progression of what tastes good to them goes from sweet to bitter. Coffee might make you gack now, but when you're in college you just may find you can't live without it. Part of coffee's appeal is medicinal (a lot of grown-ups feel it helps them

wake up in the morning) but mostly it's social. It gives them an excuse to get together and hang out, as in, "Say, if you have a little time this week, why don't you drop by for a cappuccino?" That way they don't have to come right out and say, "Hi, Miriam, it's Edna. Wanna come over and play?"

◉ **Alcohol and tobacco.** These are two more ways that people demonstrate that they've reached "adult status," or at least are dying to look cool. People who just can't wait to grow up often sample these forbidden fruits early, forcing themselves to endure the general yuckiness until they get hooked, and the authorities have to intervene.

# Tactic #5:
## Scare Your Way to Social Success

Find some ultragross pictures of the diseased lungs of former smokers or of cars crashed by drunk drivers. Then if somebody ever offers you a cigarette or a drink, whip out the photos and say, "Thanks just the same, but I have no intention of ending up like *this.*" At first you'll get a rep as being too straitlaced, but after a while other kids will start asking to see the pictures, and before you know it you will be cool. Which is even better than *looking* cool.

# 3

## THE SOUNDS OF SENIORITY
### Groans, Wheezes, Sighs, and Snores

As bodies age they start to rattle, squeak, and cough, just like old cars. And each noisy car part has its equivalent in the noisy adult: mouth equals grille, engine equals muscles, wheels equal feet, and exhaust pipe equals . . . well, let's just leave it at that.

Of course, a kid can make all the same sounds that a grown-up can, but they have specific meanings when expressed by an adult. Here are a few translations:

| Sound | Meaning | Sound | Meaning |
|-------|---------|-------|---------|
| Groan | "I knew this would happen." | Oof (medium) | "That was a huge lunch." |
| Sigh (quiet) | "That was my best tablecloth." | Oof (loud) | "Next time, warn me before you jump in my lap." |
| Sigh (loud) | "I've totally wasted my life." | | |
| Snore | "Can't we just TiVo this?" | Burp | (Trick question. You will never hear an adult burp, because all adults have mastered the art of burping silently.) |
| Wheeze | "I've gotta start working out." | | |
| Oof (quiet) | "I've gotta stop working out with barbells." | | |

# Beware the Dawn Yawn

Always be on the alert for the sound of a grown-up yawning. In the evening, this may signal your big chance to misbehave—as soon as they're asleep, the party's on! But in the *morning*, a yawn can be a sign of danger. Beware of any adult who, upon getting out of bed, yawns loudly or repeatedly. What they're really saying is, "I'm up, I'm getting old, and I ain't too happy about it." Be especially wary of "ooooowwwrrr," "eaaggh," or, in extreme cases, "uff uff uff." Offer this person a cup of coffee and then steer clear of them until after they drink it.

FAQs:
Body

Q: Why do grown-ups stay up after midnight, talking and laughing?

A: Because they can. Many adults never get used to being allowed to do things that were forbidden during childhood, and continue being "bad for badness's sake" long after ceasing to enjoy it. There are probably some kids who, if told they're not allowed to stick their heads in a bucket of cobras, would celebrate their twenty-first birthday at Chuck E. Snakes.

👁 👁 👁

Q: Why is my mom so worried about finding a gray hair?

A: Hair gets its color from a chemical called melanin, which is produced in pigment cells that live in hair follicles. As the cells eventually die off, less melanin is produced, which means less color, which means more gray. Some folks never have to face this problem, though, because they get regular visits from the Clairol Fairy or the Grecian Formula Genie.

Q: Why does my grandma keep getting Botox injections? I think she looked fine before.

A: Your grandma wants to look like the "ageless" celebrities she sees on TV. Trouble is, if she overdoes the shots she won't be able to move her face muscles anymore, and the only way you'll know whether she's happy or sad is by asking her. Those TV celebrities are bad role models for your grandmother. Try hiding the remote.

☻ ☻ ☻

Q: Why are they always forgetting things?

A: A grown-up's mind is like an overstuffed closet, only instead of brooms and raincoats, it's jammed with every single thing they've ever seen, heard, said, or thought. Nothing gets permanently lost in there, but with each passing year it takes a little longer to locate any given item.

It's interesting, however, to note which things are *hard* for them to remember (like the pet iguana they promised you if you cleaned out the attic) and which things are *easy* (like the bowling ball you dropped on their foot when you were seven).

Adults are constantly looking for lost objects, mostly car keys and glasses. Then when the object finally turns up, they say, "Why is it always in the last place I look?"

To which you could reply, "Because if it *weren't* in the last place you looked, that means you would keep looking after you'd found it, which wouldn't be very smart, would it?" But be careful if you do, or the next time *you* get lost, they might not come looking for you.

◑ ◑ ◑

**Q:** Why do they lick their fingers before turning a page?

**A:** They have to because their skin dries out and loses its traction. But it's still gross, isn't it? Consider using this disgusting behavior against them the next time they accuse *you* of poor hygiene.

◑ ◑ ◑

**Q:** Is it okay to laugh when an adult farts?

**A:** It depends on where you are. In a canoe, always. In church, never. In an elevator, just hold your breath.

# PART 2: GROWN-UPS AT HOME

*I*dentifying the grown-ups under your own roof is easy: they're the obstacles between you and everything you want, whether it's dessert before dinner or your own helicopter. In general, these people will be your parents. And unless you happen to be starring in a hit sitcom, they're the ones paying the bills . . . so they make the rules. But that doesn't mean you have to obey them.

In the following chapters, we'll first describe the major types of domesticated adults and then delve into the fine art of living with them, including such strategies as cooperation, manipulation, collaboration, and—if all of these fail—revenge.

# 4

# THE PARENT TRAP
## How Soccer Moms and Baseball Dads Ruin Your Fun, and Why

When your folks were your age they looked forward to doing all sorts of interesting, important stuff when they grew up, just like you. But with the exception of noted overachievers like Albert Einstein and Oprah Winfrey, they pretty much didn't do it. What they did instead was go into careers they'd never planned to go into (like marketing), settle down in towns they'd never heard of (like Findlay, Ohio), and give birth to *you*.

Mom's and Dad's actual chances of becoming rock stars or supercross champs may be dead and buried, but their dreams go marching on. Trouble is, the dreams often get dumped on their *kids*, along with the high pressure and hard work required to achieve them. This explains all those arm-waving, red-faced parents at soccer games, screaming themselves hoarse at your coach, the ref, or you while you're out on the field just trying to have a good time. If they can't succeed, somebody's gonna succeed, and it darn well better be *their kid*.

To put it more simply, your parents aren't trying to

ruin your fun, they're trying to *steal* it. They have a fancy word to describe this crime: *vicarious*, as in, "We're living *vicariously* through our children." Or to put a good face on it, "We just want our kids to have better lives than we did."

Yeah, so they can *steal* them.

To be fair, most parents know better than to saddle you with the responsibility of making up for their disappointing lives while you're trying to live yours, but even the best ones slip from time to time. To find out whether action must be taken against *your* parents, here's a chart. Each infraction committed by your mom or dad counts as one point:

# Adult Crimes and Misdemeanors

1. Naming you after themselves.

2. Insisting that you go into the family business, even if it's safe-cracking.

3. Photographing or videotaping every single thing you do, then filling whole shelves and websites with the results.

4. Staying in the room during your piano lesson (unless they are your piano teacher).

5. Dressing exactly like you (unless you are both on the same baseball team).

6. Driving you to and from school every day, even if there are buses available or you live less than four blocks away.

7. Screaming at your hockey coach because he doesn't give you enough playing time. (If your mom does this, count two points.)

8. Forcing you to wear your hair in a style that would look bad on you but good on them. (If your dad does this, count three points.)

9. Trying to start a band with you and your friends.

10. Using your PlayStation more than two hours at a time.

If your score is four or higher, your parents must be forced to Get a Life—before they run off with yours.

# Tactic #6:
# Defend Your Life

In milder cases, it may be enough to remind them that the Good Book says "put away childish things." (1 Corinthians 13:11. A little Bible knowledge can come in handy!) But with the hardcores, such as mothers who try on their daughter's tube tops, you'll need to get serious. Offer to switch lives with them for a day or two—if they're so crazy about youth, let 'em experience the whole enchilada, from homework to braces to not being allowed into R-rated films. Take away their driver's licenses and credit cards. If there's a holiday gathering coming up, make your folks sit at the kids' table while you eat off the good plates, crack jokes that they don't understand, and send them to bed at nine p.m. They'll get the picture and back off.

# 5

## AUNTS, UNCLES, AND OTHERS
### Family Gatherings, Goofy Gifts,
### and the Superold

These creatures frequently gather in large herds during the holidays and at reunions, where they're found grazing at buffets, nosing through photo albums, barking out stories that everyone's heard about a million times.

### Tactic #7:
### Spice It Up!

Competition is the key. Start it out friendly, and see where it leads. Try something like, "Dad, Uncle Bill thinks he can beat you at arm-wrestling, even though you're twenty pounds heavier," "Mom, why don't you and your sisters get together and figure out who's been in therapy the longest," or "Grandma, whose elbow skin sags the most, yours or Grandpa's?"

An adult's sense of maturity is strong, but old family rivalries are stronger. You should find the ensuing battles extremely amusing. And if you don't, you and your cousins can always slip away and raid the dessert table.

It can get pretty creepy hanging out with people who are a lot like you (they are, after all, your relatives) but slightly distorted. It's a little like looking at your reflection in a dark room while shining a flashlight under your chin.

Once this morbid fascination wears off, family gatherings can get dull fast. And that's when it's up to *you* to save these boring people from their boring selves.

## Gifts from Distant Family Members

Sometimes aunts, uncles, and grandparents don't know you well enough to pick out something cool, so they just take a shot in the dark. This is how unlucky kids have ended up on the receiving end of presents such as:

- Socks
- Underwear
- Matching bathrobe and slippers
- Book on stamp collecting
- Junior gardening kit
- Chia pet
- Framed baby photo of you with dumb expression on your face
- Milli Vanilli CD (If you haven't heard of this duo, check them out online. On second thought, don't.)

# Why Does Grandpa Smell Funny?

**Nose:** Stopped working many years ago (about the same time Grandpa did), leaving him unaware that he's funky.

**Armpits:** Grandma doesn't tell him to wash; her nose doesn't work, either.

**Mouth:** Cigars, whiskey, dentures.

**Clothes:** Figures washing them once a year is often enough.

**Feet:** Old socks with holes in the toes so big, he can get into them from either end.

**Whole body:** Wears English Leather cologne (which smells like neither England nor leather—what were they thinking?).

# Tactic #8:
## Dealing with the Superold

What with modern medicine keeping humans alive well into their eighties, nineties, and beyond, you're more likely than ever to encounter one of these ancient specimens. Your ability to hang tough will be taxed to the max by their splotchy skin, loose hearing-aid batteries, and random recollections of people and places you never heard of.

The important thing here is to focus on the marbles that these silly senior citizens still have left, instead of crying over the ones they lost. There are plenty of ninety-year-olds who can still play the cello, beat you at chess, and speak foreign languages, yet are liable to forget where their mouth is and stick a spoonful of mashed potatoes right in their ear. (Helpful hint: avoid mealtime visits!)

And if the geezer in question gets gloomy, the following two phrases are sure to cheer them up: "senior discount" and "early bird special."

# 6

## THE BABYSITTER
### Friend or Foe?

First of all, they shouldn't be called babysitters. You're not a baby, and you're darned well going to see to it that they spend very little of their time with you sitting. Chasing you, cleaning up your messes, and locking themselves in the bathroom is more like it. (Better job descriptions would be "Damage Control Supervisor," "Ground Marshall," "Youth Wrangler," and "Deputy Parent.")

You have three goals while under the control of these temporary wardens: (a.) have as much fun as possible; (b.) if you like the sitters, see to it that they want to return; and (c.) if you don't, make sure they *never* return.

The first thing you need to know about babysitters is that they are *snoops*. Before your folks' car is out of the driveway, your sitter will have raided the refrigerator, searched the pantry, inspected the medicine cabinet, and rifled through bookshelves for prize info about your family, which she'll later pass on to the SSNB (Secret Society of Nosy Baby-sitters). This will help her fellow Wranglers in the neighborhood know how much to charge, who has the best food, and generally how much they can get away with.

If your sitter is going to go to all that trouble, you owe it to her to (as the old song goes) "give her something to talk about." A rubber snake under the bathroom sink is a good place to start, but to make it a truly memorable evening, consider a real one.

## Tactic #9:
## Make Your Own Memo!

Once the evening is under way, be sure to spend it on *your* terms, not your folks', and *definitely* not the sitter's. Many parents will try to kill your fun with written instructions stuck to the refrigerator: bedtimes, permitted TV programs or video games, homework to be completed, etc. Put your superior computer skills to work: create your own memo and swap it for the real one. Here's a customizable version to get you started—just fill in the blanks.

**To: Babysitter**

**From: Mom + Dad**

**Re: House Rules**

[Your name] has low blood sugar, so be sure he gets plenty of [chocolate / fudge / chocolate fudge]. At least half a pound. And [sibling's name] is allergic to all green, leafy vegetables. Her doctor says that [Red Bull / Coke / milk shakes] and [Doritos / Pringles / Skittles] are a good substitute.

Both the kids are having trust issues, but you can get on their good side by doing all their [schoolwork / yardwork / chores] for them. We think it's important for them to know that they can rely on others.

[Your name] has been waking up a lot during the night, so let [him / her] stay up as late as possible, and keep him [active / happy / satisfied]. Basically let the kids do whatever they want.

If we're not back by midnight, you can go on home; the kids will be fine by themselves. Also, they're in an early-cognition [science / geography / driver's education] program, so be sure to leave the keys to the Explorer where they can easily reach them.

If everything else fails, try bringing the sitter over to your side. Deep inside, she's really just a slightly older kid who's trying desperately to be a grown-up. If you can get her to forget this for a moment and enlist her in water-balloon fights or pillow-fort building, everybody wins. At least until Mom and Dad get home.

# 7

## NEIGHBORS

### Class, Gossip, and Envy on the Street Where You Live

As an aquarium is to fish, or an ant farm is to ants, or a cave is to bats, a neighborhood is to grown-ups. Larger than a home yet smaller than a city, this is where individuals establish roots, raise families, pay taxes, and make lifelong friends—who then let their dog poop in your yard. And it is by carefully observing the adult human as it moves about its "turf" that we begin to understand its complex social relationships.

Whether city, town, or suburb, there's a lot more going on behind the shiny exteriors of every adult community than meets the eye. Here's a sampling of what's really going on, along with some ways you can benefit from it.

- **Jealousy.** Every grown-up is afraid that the family across the street has more money than they do, even if the house across the street is a dump. That's why Mom and Dad watch home-improvement shows and then knock themselves out every weekend fixing up their own dumps with paint, vinyl siding, room additions, and custom outdoor grills.

## Tactic #10:
## Keep Up with the Joneses

The simple sentence "Alex's house has a jungle gym/pool/climbing wall/riding stable" can make it *way* more likely that you'll get one, too. (On second thought, you might want to skip the riding stable—you could end up in charge of cleaning it.)

◉ **Gossip.** Just like in the schoolyard, this is a powerful weapon in the struggle for status—gossip is the vandalism of social interactions, allowing you to tear down with a few words the reputation that your neighbor spent years building up. Saying nasty things about other people behind their backs may be a sin, but that rarely stops a grown-up. (For one thing, it's much safer than saying nasty things straight to somebody's face and giving them the chance to punch you in yours.)

# Close to Home

**H**ere are some of the people in your neighborhood—
and how to deal with each.

**Grumpy Old Man:** Avoid.

**Grumpy Old Man with Water Gun:**
Purchase a raincoat.

**Frequent Loud Partiers:**
Infiltrate and observe (see
chapter 14, "Spying on Parties").

**Family with Pool:** Make
friends.

**Family with Junked Car in Front Yard:**
Make friends; they might let you use
the car as a clubhouse.

**Family with Nice Kid
Your Age:** Make friends;
declare joint war on adults.

**Family with Nice Kid
Your Age, Opposite Sex:**
Make friends; get older; go on date.

**Bullies:** Send written invitation
to dinner party, giving Grumpy
Old Man's address.

# Tactic #11:
# Double-Reverse Gossip

Go around saying *nice* things about *awful* people, right to their face. This will either (a.) force them to become nicer in order to live up to their new and improved rep; or (b.) convince them that you've gone totally mental. They'll start avoiding you, leaving you with one fewer awful person in your life.

# 8
# THE RELATIVE NATURE OF TIME
## Why Yours Drags While Theirs Flies

**K**ids and adults experience the passage of time in totally different ways.

In elementary school, how long does it take to get from one grade to the next? Forever, right? But once people get past the age of twenty-five or so, the years start flying by, and they wander around staring at the ground and muttering, "Where has the time gone?"

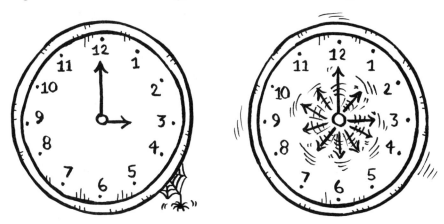

In the real, physical world, of course, clocks move at the same rate for everybody: one minute per minute.

But *psychologically*, it's a different story for adults—the minute hand seems to move as fast for them as the second hand does for you.

There are three reasons for this:

1. *A lot more happens in a kid's life than in an adult's.* During the twelve long months between the first day of third grade and the first day of fourth, an entire lifetime can be lived: friendships bloom and die; whole new subjects and skills are mastered and then forgotten; skateboarding or Harry Potter can climb or drop nine places on a kid's top-ten list. But during this same period, all your mom manages to do is buy a new wall calendar for her office, and your dad finally decides what color to stain the deck.

2. *Simple arithmetic.* If you're ten, one year makes up a whole 10 percent of your life up to now. If you're forty, one year is just—well, figure this one out yourself. Use a calculator if you must.

3. *Growth rate decreases with age.* This is why adults who haven't seen you for a while always flip out over "how tall you've gotten," while they themselves haven't grown an inch. (In fact, some grandparents *shrink* slightly).

## Tactic #12:
## Relativity to the Rescue!

The great physicist Albert Einstein once said: "Put your hand on a hot stove for a minute, and it seems like an hour. Sit with a pretty girl for an hour, and it seems like a minute. THAT'S relativity." So next time you're on a car trip with your folks that's taking forever, don't just groan the tired old lament "Are we there yet?" Instead, spring that Einstein quote on them. Even if it doesn't win their sympathy, they'll be impressed that you know who Einstein was, and just might repay you by stepping on the gas.

The way that time drags for young people but zooms past for old ones shows up in all sorts of nasty ways. For example, punishment. A parent will think nothing of grounding you for a whole weekend over some minor wrongdoing, like shaving the cat. After two bleak days of twiddling your thumbs and rearranging your sock drawer, your mind is gone and so is your will to live.

And what do your parents say to each other at breakfast on Monday, just as you're being released from your long stay in solitary confinement? "Boy, that weekend sure flew by!"

## Tactic #13:
## How Old Are They, Anyway?

Unlike trees, you can't tell a grown-up's age by cutting them down and counting the rings. With a man, simply keep asking until he tells you. But it's a bad idea to ask a *woman* her age—not because it's rude, but because she won't tell you. (Not the truth, anyway.) It's much easier to slip her purse open, sneak a peek at her driver's license, and do the math. Just don't get caught.

# 9
# NOSTALGIA
## How Their Past Affects Your Present

"Nostalgia" means "a wistful or overly sentimental yearning for some past period or irrecoverable condition," which is Adultspeak (see chapter 10, "Communication") for getting all worked up about the old days. But in the wacky world of adults, nostalgia is a little more complicated.

Parents can be extremely sneaky in the way they use nostalgia to manipulate you. When they're criticizing the music, clothes, or reading material you like, they always view their *own* earlier years as some sort of magical era when everything was good and pure and beautiful—until *your* generation came along and messed it all up. But when they're trying to get you to do something unpleasant, like shovel snow, they pull a 180 and start yakking about how tough they had it when *they* were young. Here's an example. A foot of snow fell on your driveway last night, and now your dad's trying to shame you into risking frostbite and back injury because he's too busy doing sudoku to shovel it himself. He'll probably pull something like this:

## Tactic #14:
## A Dose of Their Own Medicine

When Mom or Dad starts droning on about their past, wait till they're done, then give them your own double-barreled blast from the past.

"You don't know how good you've got it. Why, when I was your age my dad made me catch the snowflakes before they hit the ground. With tweezers! Barefoot! Then we had to bring the snow inside and melt it to make our own water, because we didn't have *fancy bottled water* like you lucky kids do . . ."

"I know what you mean. I still remember Tuesday like it was yesterday. In fact, it *was* yesterday. Man, that was some day. They don't make days like *that* anymore. Remember how good cereal tasted back then? So crispy. Now it's all stale. Maybe because I forgot to close the box. But the time passed. Suddenly it was noon. Then afternoon. Then *late* afternoon. Those were hard times. You wouldn't remember them. You were at work. But we kept it together. Me and the sitter. Then, practically without warning, it was dinnertime. The world had changed. It was a darker place. And yet brighter in a way, because the lights were on . . . "

# 10

## COMMUNICATION
### What They Say, and What It Really Means

You can always tell how old people are by how they talk—the greater the age, the longer the word. (Just look at the title of this chapter—a kid would've called it "Talking.")

Grown-ups use complicated, fancy-sounding language to show off how sophisticated (cool) and perspicacious (smart) they are, particularly if they're trying to hide something. For example, ask a politician if he took a bribe, and he'll come out with something like, "At this particular juncture in time I am neither willing nor under any obligation to respond to this inquisition." Ask a kid if she broke a vase, and what do you get? "Not telling."

A few perfectly intelligent adults don't talk in this crazy, roundabout way. They say what they mean, and they mean what they say. But most don't, so it's absolutely essential that you learn to understand "Adultspeak" in order to (a.) know what's going on, and (b.) avoid falling into the trap of using it yourself.

Here's a little dictionary of adult words and phrases, and their "Kidspeak" translations. Look carefully and you'll see the adult with the fancy phrase is usually trying to sound important, trying to trick you, or just plain fibbing.

## Adultspeak Dictionary

| Grown-Up | Kid | Grown-Up | Kid |
|---|---|---|---|
| Residence | House | Exponential | Big |
| Vehicle | Car, truck | Prior to | Before |
| Customer Care Specialist | Salesman | Subsequent to | After |
| Account Executive | Salesman | Reiterate | Repeat |
| Incarcerated | In jail | Hydrate | Drink water |
| Exonerated | Out of jail | Cutting-edge | New |
| Positively impact | Help | State-of-the-art | New |
| Negatively impact | Hurt | At this particular juncture | Now |
| Challenge | Scary problem | Let me think about it | No |
| Concerned | Scared | | |

# 11
## BUTT-KISSING AND BROWN-NOSING
### How to Get on a Grown-Up's Good Side, at Least Temporarily

There's nothing wrong with complimenting Mom's outfit or Dad's haircut, but if you seriously want to get out of the doghouse for a past offense (or lay the groundwork for a future one), you'll need:

## Tactic #15:
## The Unexpected Good Deed

Next time your father comes home from work looking exhausted, hand him a cold beer and hit him right between the eyes with "Guess what, Dad? I raked the leaves so you wouldn't have to." Then check out the smile on his face. You can double the impact with "Dad, I finished up my homework early, so I raked the leaves." Or, to really swing for the fences, try "I finished up my homework early, so I raked the leaves. *Is there anything else I could do for you?*" (Use this last one with care—he might ask you to clean out the garage.)

Note the key element of *surprise*. If Dad expected you to rake the yard (which he would have indicated by nagging you to do it every day for the past week), your good deed wouldn't pack nearly the same punch. Also bear in mind that this kind of stunt can backfire and mark you as a snot-nosed little butt-kisser among your siblings—which, of course, you are. One way out of this is to share credit for the deed with your big sister ("[Sister's name] and I raked the leaves . . .") or even handing it over altogether ("[Sister's name] raked the leaves"). You'll still get partial credit for being the bearer of good news, and if your sister has any class at all, she'll return the favor someday.

Once you've made several deposits in the PFB (Parental Favor Bank) and let the interest add up for

a month or two, it's time to cash in. (Note: this waiting period is *extremely important*. If you ask for a new puppy on the same day you surprised Mom by cleaning her bathtub, she'll see right through your scheme and never buy you anything again.)

# Seven Good Deeds and What to Expect in Return

| Deed | Reward (Approximated) |
|---|---|
| 1. Empty kitchen trash | Pat on head |
| 2. Same, plus replace plastic liner | Extralarge dessert |
| 3. Same, plus wash can out with Pine-Sol | Second dessert |
| 4. Make own bed | Grateful smile |
| 5. Make parents' bed | Permission to stay up extra hour (Note: be sure parents aren't in bed) |
| 6. Wash car | Ball game tickets |
| 7. Change oil, rotate tires | Ball game tickets (behind home plate) |

The important thing to remember here is that (a.) actions speak louder than words, and (b.) trying is more important than succeeding.

# 12
## MONEY (PART 1)
### How to Negotiate an Allowance

Sure, a family runs on peace, love, and understanding, but it also runs on *money*, just like a business. And in business, people get ahead by arguing, trading, compromising—in a word, *negotiating*. Let's examine a simple request for an allowance increase, taking it step by step.

## How to Negotiate a Negotiation

**Step 1: Know Your Territory.** Every family member wants something that another family member has, and *vice versa*. You want more money; your parents want to be left alone. Make it clear that they won't get what they want until you get what *you* want, even if means pitching a tent in their bedroom.

**Step 2: Evaluate your position.** Is your request reasonable? Of course it is, or you wouldn't be making it. Have you chosen the right time to ask? (Good time: after Mom gets a raise at work. Bad time: after you flunk a test.) Have you done enough butt-kissing and brown-nosing? If not, go back to chapter 11.

**Step 3: Approach the weaker parent first.** Usually Dad, although this varies. They'll want to know what you intend to do with the extra cash. Tell them you're saving up for something, so you'll look responsible and mature. (You don't have to tell them that what you're saving up for is a personal submarine.)

**Step 4: Let them make the first move.** They'll ask how big an increase you have in mind. You only want 25 percent, but ask for *double that*. When they regain consciousness, follow up with "Well, I guess we could split the difference. Maybe a 25 percent bump would be fair." (This is known as a "fallback position.") This will make them think of you as not only mature but reasonable. If they say yes, **go to the bottom**. If they say no, go to

**Step 5: Run straight to Parent B.** (In the case of single-parent households, a rich aunt or uncle may be substituted.) Repeat steps 1-4. If Parent B says yes, **go to the bottom**.

> If B says no, it's back to A, who will send you back to B, and before long you'll feel like a hockey puck. If this happens, don't panic. Cool off for a few days, then

**Step 6: Bring out the big guns.** Arrange to have your parents walk in on you while you're reading the "Help Wanted" ads in the paper, circling the most dangerous jobs—coal miner, crane operator, bomb defuser. They'll think you're insane. Tell them you've decided to drop out of school and get a head start in today's tough job market. (Use those exact words: "tough job market.") Realizing that their cheapness might actually require you to go hundreds of feet underground and blast out seams of coal will shake them up a bit. When you see that your words have taken effect, ask them one final time for the 50 percent increase. They'll offer you 25 percent. **Take it.**

**Step 7: YOU WIN!**

Note: if you do use the "Help Wanted" technique, be sure not to mention any jobs that you have the slightest chance of actually getting. You could easily find yourself delivering newspapers at 5 a.m.

# 13

# FUN THINGS YOU CAN DO WITH ADULTS

## Turning Time into "Quality Time"

For a lot of kids, having to spend time with the folks falls one step below cleaning out the cat's litter box. Parents employ two methods of torture, both unbearable: 1.) They make you do stuff *they* like, such as organizing stamp collections or comparing wallpaper samples; or 2.) They make you do stuff they think *you'll* like, such as playing board games that were already lame when they were kids (like Parcheesi and Candy Land). This presents a delicate situation. On the one hand, your aged relatives are "reaching out to you"—or at least making an attempt—and if you keep blowing them off they'll eventually stop offering to do *anything* with you, including cool stuff like taking you to water parks or go-kart tracks. On the other hand, if you're *too* cooperative you could end up spending the day at a textile museum. Once again, the key here is to *seize control*. In fact, with the right approach your Paternal and Maternal Units can provide an amusing—or even educational—form of entertainment. Here are some tips:

## Tactic #16:
## Common Ground

Because older and younger people have such different skills, opportunities to teach and learn pop up all the time. Sometimes you'll be the student, others the teacher. For example, you were practically born knowing how to set up a wireless computer network, but believe it or not, many people over forty are totally helpless at anything technical. Exploit your superiority! Show your dad how to recover an important e-mail that he accidentally deleted, and you'll be a god in his eyes. You won't always be the teacher, of course. Despite their limitations, many parents actually *do* have areas of expertise that they'll be happy to pass on to you, which will pay off big-time later in life. Here are a few:

| Skill | Your Payoff |
|---|---|
| Driving | Independence |
| Sewing on buttons | Keeping your pants up |
| Cooking | Avoiding terrible college cafeterias |
| Playing poker | World poker championship, if you're good enough |
| Making tons of money | Making tons of money |

# Tactic #17:
# Friendly Competition

As pointed out in chapter 5, competitive interfamily events are another fun way to kill a few hours when rainy weather or a power outage forces you into close quarters. Only, here, you yourself will be competing. Be sure to choose contests where you'll have a natural advantage—if you're going *mano a mano* with a parent twice your size, don't make the common mistake of fighting fair!

Here's a Domestic Decathlon. See if you can circle the likely winner of each event.

You should easily win events #1-5, and #10 of course is a slam dunk. The PUs will win #8, unless you're some kind of math whiz. #6 and #7 could go either way—some parents are *experts* at being in a bad mood, and what's worse, blaming it on you. #9 was a trick question. No matter who does a better job of vacuuming, your *parents* win, because now the house is vacuumed, isn't it?

| Event | Projected Winner | |
|---|---|---|
| 1. Hiding | You | Parental Units |
| 2. Getting dirty | You | Parental Units |
| 3. Screaming (loudest) | You | Parental Units |
| 4. Screaming (longest) | You | Parental Units |
| 5. Stare-down | You | Parental Units |
| 6. Pouting | You | Parental Units |
| 7. Sulking | You | Parental Units |
| 8. Working out family budget | You | Parental Units |
| 9. Vacuuming | You | Parental Units |
| 10. Armpit farts | You | Parental Units |

Results:

# 14
## SPYING ON PARTIES
### Gathering Data While Avoiding Detection

The absolute top, best, *numero uno* place to behold the adult human in all its natural glory is at a social gathering. Whether draped in full bling at a fancy dinner party or kicking back at a backyard barbecue, here is where *Adultus Americanus* can be seen getting down, getting funky, and on certain special occasions, getting loose.

Your job is to slip into these scenes unobserved and *observe observe observe*. Ideal hiding places are behind stair railings, under couches, inside coat closets, and if necessary out in the yard, through binoculars (although this cuts down on your ability to hear what's going on).

It's best to work in pairs, with a friend or sibling as a partner, so you can take turns acting as lookouts and then compare notes afterward. Also, when you get busted for spying (and you *will* get busted), you can divide the blame by two.

Here's a diagram of a typical house, organized by what you're likely to see in each room.

**Den: Jokes.** "Adult-style" joke-telling is a lot like the kid version, only when an adult doesn't get a joke, he'll laugh anyway because he's too embarrassed to admit he doesn't get it. You can prove this by telling a joke that makes absolutely no sense to a group of four adults. At least three of them will crack up.

**Family Room: Nonverbal communication.** To communicate privately in public places, adults use a complicated system of signs and gestures, sort of like a third-base coach giving a base runner the "steal" signal.) The wife in this picture is telling her husband, "You are *so* in trouble."

**Kitchen: Verbal communication.** Polite adults avoid politics and religion in conversation, which is too bad, because those two topics spark the liveliest debates. Want proof? Before the party, place a Bible, Torah, and Koran on the table. Then sit back and wait for the fun to begin.

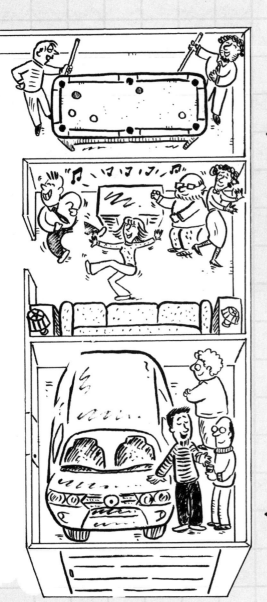

**Rec Room: Fun and games.** In a sporting contest, the two sides start out theoretically equal but end up unequal, leaving one to celebrate and the other to sulk. Considering how many adult friendships have ended over a "friendly" game of darts, pool, or cards, this should probably be called the "wreck room."

**Living Room: Dancing.** Unless you happen to be in a room full of professionals, the best way to watch grown-ups dance is with your eyes closed.

**Garage: Bragging.** Also known as boasting, fronting, blowing smoke, talking big, and selling wolf tickets. An adult who can't stop talking about his huge car, huge house, or huge bank account is often making up for his tiny opinion of himself.

# Tactic #18:
# Showbiz Kids

The easiest way to get invited to a Real Adult Party is to be asked to entertain. If you've developed a knack for playing an instrument, telling jokes, or doing magic tricks, you may be allowed to stay up so your folks can display you like a trained circus dog. Putting on a *great* show might even score you an agent.

# 15
## HOW TO DRIVE YOUR PARENTS NUTS
### A Truckload of Treacherous Tricks

If you've followed the steps laid out in this book so far, you probably have the adults in your home fairly well under control by now. But grown-ups, like crocodiles, are unpredictable. If you've tried everything and gotten nowhere, you're left with only one alternative: revenge.

Many so-called "experts" on childhood believe that minor acts of mischief, such as mooning, toilet papering houses, and that Midwestern favorite, cow tipping, are just part of growing up, and should therefore be—if not encouraged— at least tolerated.

So far, so good. But if you've learned nothing else, it's that you should *never* do what an adult expects. To put it bluntly, if you're going to wreak havoc, show a little imagination. Maybe something along these lines:

## Tactic #19: Fight Dirty

**A.** Secretly learn French. When you have it securely under your belt, suddenly start speaking *only* French in your home. Demand to watch only subtitled movies and laugh at every joke right before your parents do. For maximum impact, teach a brother or sister French, too, and say scandalous things about your parents right in front of them.

**B.** Do things that are harmless but utterly pointless. Put everything in the kitchen in alphabetical order, from aprons to zucchini; mail a letter to your dad's work address asking him what time it is; call relatives you haven't spoken to in years and ask them if they prefer Coke or Pepsi. This will gain you a rep as an eccentric, and your parents will start writing down everything you do so that when you get famous, they'll be able to say, "I knew there was something special about my kid when she gave names to all the tiles on the bathroom floor."

C. If your parents are going out for the evening, set your mom's watch five minutes fast and your dad's five minutes slow. Then *she* can yell at *him* for taking too long to get ready (for a change).

D. Pepper your conversation with words and names that sound naughty but aren't, such as:

| Word | Meaning | Word | Meaning |
|------|---------|------|---------|
| abreast | aware of | nuptial | relating to a marriage ceremony |
| anise | licorice-like spice | pustule | inflamed skin bump |
| Balzac | French novelist, 1799–1850 | titillate | excite |
| buttress | building wall support | and, finally . . . | |
| circumvent | avoid by going around | pupu platter | assortment of appetizers found in some Asian restaurants |
| gland | gland | | |
| masticate | chew | | |

**Q:** How can I stop my parents from embarrassing me by trying to act younger than they are?

**A:** By acting older than *you* are. Develop a taste for brussels sprouts. Strike up conversations with insurance agents. Use words like "responsibility" and "foodstuffs." Read the business section of the newspaper, circling articles about public transit and trade deficits, and ask them questions like, "Is your portfolio sufficiently diversified?" or "What's your five-year fiscal plan?" This should shock your folks into acting their age. Plus, your father might make you a partner in his firm.

☺   ☺   ☺

**Q:** Why is my mom's purse so heavy?

**A:** You probably already know what's in your mom's purse, because you've been through it a dozen times. What you're *really* asking is, "What could possibly be so important to an adult female that she'll risk permanent spine damage to lug it around?"

All girls know the answer to this question (in fact, they're born with it), but *no boys do*—nor will they ever learn it as men, no matter how often their wives explain it to them. Actually, the very fact that you asked indicates that you're a boy. In which case, it's none of your business.

⚫ ⚫ ⚫

**Q:** Why do my mom and dad like to take naps? I hate naps.

**A:** One of two reasons:

1.) They're exhausted from keeping up with you, which proves that you're doing your job. Keep it up.

2.) They just want some time away from you. This doesn't mean they don't love you, just that you get on their nerves now and then, which *also* proves you're doing your job. If they wanted something boring and predictable around the house, they wouldn't have had kids, they would've bought an aquarium.

⚫ ⚫ ⚫

**Q:** Why do they hug and kiss me all the time?

**A:** You didn't include a picture, so let's assume it's because you're so darned adorable. The best defense against this method of attack is to grow into an awkward, sulking teenager.

The whole subject of social bodily contact among adults almost deserves its own book. Women like hugging men and other women; men like hugging women but usually not other men, except right after the Super Bowl. (Note: this must include violent back-pounding.)

👁 👁 👁

**Q:** My biggest sister is eight years older than me and she acts like she's my mom. What should I do?

**A:** Demand an allowance.

# PART 3:
# GROWN-UPS
# AT SCHOOL

**N**ews flash! Teachers don't spend their nonteaching hours hibernating in sealed pods. Most actually enjoy rich, varied lives. (Some have even been known to water ski!)

But this section isn't "all teachers, all the time." Throughout America's schools, entire armies of highly trained adults are striving right now toward the same goal: to turn you into a well-behaved, productive member of society—although it's unclear how offering you greasy meat loaf and limp pizza in the cafeteria will accomplish this.

# 16
## THE THREE RS
### Reading, wRiting, and bRibery

It takes all sorts of grown-ups to run a school, but the main sort you'll be dealing with in the near future is, of course, teachers. And as in most interactions with adults, you can get what you want by giving them what they want . . . within reason, of course.

What do teachers want? Believe it or not, most of the time they want their students to learn things. But occasionally a teacher will consider it a victory just to get rid of them. We've all encountered a student whose very presence in a classroom is so disruptive that a teacher will be tempted to promote him or her (usually him) to the next grade just to be free of the little beast. In fact, this student may be you. If so, consider sending this teacher a sympathy card later in life, or if you can afford it, a few bucks.

Some teachers are so obviously in the wrong career (they're the ones who, when the afternoon bell rings, actually beat the students out the door) that they should be gently nudged toward a more appropriate one. Try leaving pamphlets on your teacher's desk with names like "Careers in Accordion Repair" or "Is Meat Cutting for You?" Or write a report on poor pay and lousy conditions in the education field, followed by another about the excellent starting salaries for chemical engineers in foreign countries. They'll get the hint.

On the other hand, teachers who do a good job should be rewarded, and not just because it's The Nice Thing to Do—it's how you train them. Education is a two-way street, and doing a nice turn for a teacher who actually teaches you something useful or steers you toward a stupendous book (like this one, though that's unlikely) can be as effective as tossing a doggie treat to a schnauzer who has learned to sit up and beg.

## Tactic #20:
## Show Your Appreciation!

Although giving your teacher an apple won't have much effect these days (unless it's an Apple computer), slipping her a twenty on the first day of class should at least get you a choice seat. But the best way to show gratitude to good teachers is to be a good *student*—make an effort to stay awake during boring subjects, don't talk in class or flood the bathroom, don't sue them unless they really deserve it, blah blah blah. Not a very fresh approach but guaranteed to work.

# What Teachers Get vs. What They Really Want

| Get | Want |
|---|---|
| Coffee mug | Italian espresso machine |
| Decorative pillow | Extra hour of sleep |
| Bubble gum | Bubble bath |
| Earrings | Earplugs |
| Stationery set | You, stationary in your seat |
| Chocolate-colored scarf | Chocolate they can scarf down |
| McDonald's gift certificate | McDonald's stock certificate |

# What to Do if You See Your Teacher Outside of School

It's always slightly upsetting to spot a teacher who has strayed from their regular domain. It's out of context, like hearing your mom sing karaoke or seeing the president in plaid shorts.

Don't fall apart, just follow this chart.

| If Your Teacher Is . . . | You Should . . . |
|---|---|
| . . . walking down the street, | . . . say hi. |
| . . . shopping, | . . . say hi, unless teacher is buying something embarrassing, like a toilet brush. |
| . . . eating in a restaurant, | . . . send over a dessert with a note reading, "Compliments of the Class of 2018." |
| . . . about to get hit in the face by a pie, | . . . jump in and take it in the face yourself. You'll look great on YouTube. |
| . . . talking loudly during a movie, | . . . yell, "Quiet, please." Then duck. |
| . . . kissing someone passionately, | . . . duck, then yell, "Get a room!" |

# 17
## TYPES OF TEACHERS
### Classifying the Head of the Class

The number of species of teachers is incredibly large—nearly as large, in fact, as the number of species of beetles. (The two groups are easy to tell apart: beetles can be identified by their hard, shiny exoskeletons; teachers, by their large collections of dry-erase markers.) By the time you've finished your education you will have been exposed to the whole range, all the way from award-winning scholars to psychos who should be kept in leather restraints. Here are a few of the major types:

**The "Commander."** This person really belongs in front of an army, not a whiteboard. Uniformity, not education, is the Commander's goal, and if by the end of the year the class has learned nothing, at least they've all learned the *exact* same nothing, and the Commander is happy.

**The "Fanatic."** When these nut jobs start yakking on and on about something that they love but you simply can't get into (like cell mitosis or California's historic missions), you can still benefit from your time together by using it to practice looking fascinated when you're actually bored to tears. This skill will come in handy in adult life: your boss's fishing trip, your sister-in-law's wedding photos, political speeches . . . you'll have to live through all of these marathons at some point, so you might as well start training now.

**The "Best Friend."** Like the overly involved parents we met in Chapter 4, the Best Friend is trying to make up for missed childhood experiences by muscling in on yours. This is fine up to a point—a teacher who'll join in a dodgeball game or mix up pottery clay with her bare feet reminds us that there's such a thing as a cool adult—but if they start getting *too* chummy, such as asking to share your cupcake, brush them back with a high, hard pitch: "I have all the friends I need, thanks. What I'm looking for is a good, solid role model."

**The "Cryptkeeper."** Every school seems to be required by law to hire one teacher who's got a wrinkle for every student she ever yelled at. Don't be too quick to dismiss these cobwebbed relics. They can actually teach you a lot—especially about ancient history, since they were there for so much of it.

But it's bad form to organize a schoolwide betting pool, with a prize going to the person who correctly predicts the date of the Cryptkeeper's forced retirement. And if he or she finds out about the pool before that date arrives, you might be amazed by how fast they can move.

**"I, Robot."** This cyborg has been teaching the same subject at the same grade level for so long that it (we might as well as call it an "it," because Robots exhibit few human characteristics) now dispenses identical, flavorless packets of information as mechanically as a gumball machine. Its chosen specialty is almost always one that doesn't change from year to year, like geometry. If I, Robot stays in the same place too long, it'll either rust or go on a rampage. In the first case you'll need an oilcan; in the second, a shortcut to the nearest exit.

**"Coach."** This red-faced slab of pure energy is either an
actual phys-ed teacher or somebody who can't resist
bringing the methods of the athletic field into the
classroom—for example, by staging a spelling bee
where missing a word means doing one hundred
push-ups.

Years of screaming at athletes across stadiums or
echoing gyms have given Coach a voice louder than a jet
engine and a vocabulary like a sportscaster's. He can
use the words "compete," "competitive," and "competition"
all in the same sentence and not even notice it.

# Dark Tales from the Teachers' Lounge
## What Do They Do in There, Anyway?

**E**ver since the Stone Age, kids have wondered what goes on within the depths of these murky, intriguing, off-limits lairs. Here's the inside scoop.

It's useful to think of a teachers' lounge as a locker room at halftime. And they will never, ever, let you enter. It may seem unfair for teachers to bar students from their "inner sanctums," but if you think about it, you have no more right to go in there than the coach of the New England Patriots has to waltz into the Jets' locker room and steal *their* plays.

Training table featuring gourmet dishes much tastier than the mystery meat you get in the cafeteria

Coffee, energy drinks, and protein bars to give them the strength and stamina that you already have

Trainers icing down aching muscles for return to field (classroom)

Chalk talk laying out strategies for *running* things, *tackling* dull subjects, and *blocking* angry calls from parents

Lockers full of the more stylish clothing they wear in their real lives

Coach (principal) begging star teacher to stick around for one more season despite repeated injuries to ego, dignity

Showers for rinsing off chalk, tempera paint, gum, goo, and your germs

# 18

## SUBSTITUTES

### How to Behave Around Someone You Will Almost Certainly Never See Again

Like teachers, substitutes come in many varieties—from witty and engaging to totally unqualified. In fact, they're even more varied than regular teachers, because in most states subs don't require any special training—all they need is a college degree (in any subject!) and a pulse.

Don't misunderstand; that doesn't mean you should "accept no substitutes." Before taking action, make sure your sub is unworthy of your attention, let alone your cooperation. Telltale signs of "subpar substitutes" may include sunglasses worn indoors, a guitar case, and frequent cell phone calls to someone named "Dude." If you're still not sure, give the sub a pop quiz. Ask them to point out Dubai on a map, or to add two three-digit numbers in their head. (Make sure you know the answer first.)

Once you're convinced that this so-called "educator" has no respect for education . . . it's on.

# Tactic #21:
# Three Ways to Sink a Sub

**A.** **Don't use your real name.** This is your chance to try out an alias, and the more outlandish the better. Make one up, or choose from the following classics:

Ben Dover          I. M. Boring          Anita Bath
Oliver Klozoff      Chris P. Bacon       Claire Anett
Amanda Huggenkiss  Hugo Gurl            Chuck Waggon

If you already happen to possess a genuinely unusual name, such as "Megawati Sukarnoputri" (first woman president of Indonesia!), you're in luck. Every sub will look like an absolute idiot trying to pronounce it, and you don't even have to lie. How cool is that?

**B.** **Glue everything in the room to the ceiling** and then strap yourself into your chairs. When the sub enters, she'll think she's upside down. (Okay, so this one's impossible. But wouldn't it look cool?)

Ꮯ. **Always answer the sub's question with another question,** and insist that they do the same. The first one to make a statement loses a point and has to sit in the corner. This will not only sharpen everyone's verbal skills, but can lead to some lively exchanges, such as:

As you might expect, some adults are very good at this game, so you might want to practice a little in advance.

# 19
## TEACHER'S PET OR TEACHER'S PEST
### Which Should You Be?

Many students are perfectly happy to blend in with the crowd and sail through school unnoticed. But for those who insist on making a mark, nabbing one of these two prize slots is a good place to start.

Both jobs have advantages. Naturally, a lot depends on the teacher's personality. Before starting a new school year, interview *last* year's pet. Did this person get extra attention and easy assignments or more responsibility—and more work? Being your teacher's darling can easily start out as a blessing but end up with you staying after school to help grade papers or, if you're good at math, balance their checkbook.

If this role isn't for you, maybe the *pest* way is the best way.

Back in the bad old days, when severe punishments were allowed (such as public beatings or having to read a book called *Atlas Shrugged*), this was a risky move. You had to be 100 percent sure that there was more to gain than to lose by making a nuisance of yourself, such as building up your rep as a fearless renegade. Nowadays, the worst they can give you is a trip to the principal's office (see chapter 20).

# Pet or Pest

Here's a simple chart to help you figure out which type of classroom personality fits you best. Which behavior appeals more to you?

| Situation | "Pet" Behavior | "Pest" Behavior |
| --- | --- | --- |

**Arrival**

**Greeting**

Good morning, Ms. Karpfinger!

Zzzzzz...

| Situation | "Pet" Behavior | "Pest" Behavior |
|---|---|---|

**Homework**

**At whiteboard**

| Situation | "Pet" Behavior | "Pest" Behavior |
|---|---|---|

If most of your selections were from the first column, you may have a bright future in business, international relations, or social work. If they came from the second column, you're more likely to wind up in jail or show business.

# 20
# PRINCIPALS AND VICE PRINCIPALS
## Your Introduction to the
## "Good Cop/Bad Cop" Routine

As the top dog, big cheese, and head honcho of your school, the principal has many responsibilities. These range from making the same speech year after year at graduation ceremonies to dealing with angry parents who want to know why their daughter came home with a skin disease rarely found outside of Cambodia.

But the main way—possibly the *only* way—that a principal will ever directly touch your life is in the area of discipline.

"The principal's office." Even years after you've graduated, the very phrase will send icy fingers up and down your spine. Believe it or not, the *principal* is sometimes afraid to go to the principal's office, and this person is—you know—the principal.

Principals generally don't work alone. Helping them reach their impossible dream of maintaining order among hundreds of crazed beasts like you is the vice principal.

These "partners in crime prevention" often have

opposite personalities. If the principal is a feared disciplinarian, the vice principal will be the best friend you could ever have. If the VP has a pointy tail and breathes fire, the P will be a cream puff.

The mismatching doesn't happen by accident—these odd couples are deliberately paired in order to trap *you* into confessing crimes by shuttling you back and forth in what's known in police circles as the "good cop/bad cop" routine. Here's how it works:

Your courage is admirable (so is your familiarity with old gangster-movie slang), but this kind of bravado won't get you anywhere. Violating Civil code 56.903(a) ("No toilets on the roof") is a serious charge, and you're looking at three to five months in the slammer (study hall) unless you get yourself a good lawyer, and fast.

# 21

## LIBRARIANS

### The Best Friend You'll Ever Have Who Tells You to Shut Up

All librarians are crazy, but they're crazy in the coolest possible way: they're crazy about books. They even go to conferences all over the state, where they talk with other librarians for hours about how much they LOOOOOOOOOOOOVE books.

They also love knowledge, which makes them *extremely* valuable when your report on Indonesian wind farming is due tomorrow and you've never even heard of Indonesia. They don't know everything, but they know something just as valuable: how to *find out* everything. Even the mighty Internet can't touch the average librarian's knack for coming up with just the book you need or want or simply ought to read because they know you'll just LOOOOOOOOOOOOVE it.

## Tactic #22:
## Four Simple Rules for
## Winning Over Your Librarian

1. Don't return books late.
2. Don't spill Coke on the books, write in them, or break the binding by smushing it flat to hold your place.
3. Don't pop or crack your gum or knuckles in the library. (This is a tough one, because it sounds so cool in a big, quiet room.)
4. If you liked a book, tell the librarian. If you didn't, complain! This is how they find out what's good and what stinks.
5. Grow up, write a bestseller, and send the librarian a signed copy with the inscription, "For (name), who taught me to LOOOOOOOOOOOOOVE books."

# 22
## OTHER WORKERS
### Hairnets, Brooms, and Buses—
### the Unsung Heroes of Your School

Your Educational Support Staff (Adultspeak for "nonteachers") includes a number of highly trained grown-ups whose job is to keep your school running smoothly no matter how hard you try to cause mayhem. These employees might not have as big an impact on your life as the ones who spend their days stuffing you with knowledge like a Thanksgiving turkey, but they deserve your appreciation all the same. Besides, you just might become one someday! Here's a brief tour:

**Nurses** are responsible for, among other things, the all-important job of patching you up after an accident or illness so you can get back on your feet and into another wreck. Many school infirmaries feature windows that open onto hallways, allowing your fellow students to peek in and estimate the seriousness of your injury or disease. Don't let them down! Practice writhing in pain at home until it looks totally convincing. Or if you want even greater sympathy, learn to fake unconsciousness. Just don't make it *too* convincing, or the nurse may pump your stomach or slam a defibrillator on your chest.

**Janitors,** who sometimes prefer to be called "custodians" or "sanitary engineers," range from the friendly to the psychotic. Their skill with a mop and bucket will come in handy after food fights, stomach flu episodes, and chemistry lab explosions. Be very nice to them—for example, occasionally pick up a piece of trash and throw it in the can (being sure, of course, that the janitor sees you do it).

**Bus drivers** are among the few adults you'll meet in school who actually hold your life in their hands (the others being cafeteria cooks). Considering that these brave "earth pilots" must steer their smoke-belching, 25,000-pound yellow torpedoes through heavy traffic, day after day, in all kinds of weather, while dealing with crazed drivers outside the bus and rowdy students like you inside, it's a miracle that they don't simply snap, start babbling incoherently, and hurl themselves out the window.

In short, bus drivers deserve your greatest respect and cooperation. They also know the funniest jokes. (Just don't ask them to tell you any while the bus is in motion.)

**FAQs: School**

**Q:** Why do grown-ups always say school is so important when half the things we learn we'll never need to know to make money or get ahead in the world?

**A:** Great question. You're right; half the stuff you learn will be of no use whatsoever. The trouble is, until you're actually in midcareer you won't know *which* half.

❂  ❂  ❂

**Q:** Do teachers lecture random people on the street like they do their students?

**A:** No, but only because if they did, they'd have to give them tests afterward.

❂  ❂  ❂

**Q:** Why do parents always ask you, "How was school?"

**A:** Because they can't think of anything else to say. Even worse, they frequently tune out and don't listen to your answer.

Next time a grown-up asks you that rather dull

question, say, "It was great! Aliens landed and ate the gym teacher's head, and Hannah Driskill told every-body she was really a boy. Then we went on a field trip to Fort Knox, and they gave us each a solid-gold bar, only I traded mine for some raisins. Oh, and from now on all our classes are going to be taught in Pig Latin. And, *ow-hay as-way ork-way?*"

☺ ☺ ☺

**Q:** What should I do when my school brings in a grown-up to talk about careers and stuff?

**A:** Ask the grown-up how much money they make. If they stammer or get evasive, don't let up. Tell them you're considering going into trout farming (or whatever it is that they do) yourself, and you want to be armed with all the facts before you make such an important decision. If they *still* don't come across with the info, volunteer to help them carry their stuff out to the parking lot after-ward, and get a good look at their car. If it's more than ten years old, consider other career choices.

☺ ☺ ☺

**Q:** Do teachers ever try to embarrass us just for fun?

**A:** No, that would be mean. But when you do some-thing really embarrassing, they tell the other teachers about it in the teachers' lounge and laugh their heads off. They will deny this if you ask them.

●    ●    ●

**Q:** I live in a little town with only one school, and my mom is my teacher. What should I do?

**A:** This is tricky, because (a.) you can't complain about your mom to your teacher; (b.) you can't complain about your teacher to your mom; and (c.) if she goes easy on you at school, it'll look like "special treatment," so she'll probably go *extra* hard on you; (d.) she'll see through your "my dog ate my homework" excuse because she knows you don't have a dog.

Your best bet is to try to think of your mom as two separate people and to treat them totally differently until you drive her to the edge of madness. But if she starts talking to herself, don't assume you've succeeded—she might just be having a parent/teacher conference.

# PART 4:
# GROWN-UPS IN
# THE WILD

*I*n *the jungles of the workplace; at the watering holes of
the mall; on the rolling meadows of the golf course—it is
in these untamed spaces that this magnificent creature truly
roams free. Let's tag along and observe the many ways that
adults work, play, and spend whatever money is left over after
they pay for your food, clothing, shelter, and piano lessons.*

# 23

## WORK AND PLAY

### Are They the Same Thing?

They may sound like opposites, but to a grown-up they're really not. If you need convincing, spend a few minutes talking to an adult about their job. You'll hear terms that a kid would associate with fun and games: "Their company was in play . . . she painted me a picture . . . we're on a buying spree . . . the market's been a real roller coaster lately." (Baseball alone gives us "I hit that presentation out of the park . . . she really threw me a curve ball . . . better cover your bases . . . I need to step up to the plate.")

Even the outer layer of clothing traditionally worn by men in business settings is called a "sports coat." Nobody knows why—every sport is made harder by wearing a sports coat, especially water polo.

The work/play connection can easily be explained by the following equation:

$$\textbf{WORK} = \textbf{PLAY} + \textbf{TIME}$$

In other words, the skills you develop on the soccer field, basketball court, even *Grand Theft Auto*—okay, not *Grand Theft Auto*—will, over the years, grow into the tools you use to get ahead in adult life. Watching, learning, arguing, reasoning, persevering, thinking, negotiating—even making up crazy stories to get out of trouble—are the stuff of which great careers are made.

There are parallels between work and school as well. The workplace is actually a lot like a classroom, only with paychecks instead of report cards:

Graduation = promotion

Students from other schools = competitors

Principal = boss

Recess = coffee break

Plus, an adult version of everybody you knew in elementary school will be turning up at your workplace: the Class Clown, the Snitch, the Gossip, the Braggart, the Teacher's Pet, the School Bully, the Screwup. They'll be bigger, stronger, smarter, and possibly meaner than they are now . . . but so will you. So the better you get at dealing with them now, the better chance you'll have later on of clawing your way to the top of the heap and staying there.

# Do's and Don'ts on "Take Your Kid to Work" Day

This custom isn't as common as it used to be, but with any luck you'll be allowed at some point to visit the location where your parental figures put in their forty hours a week. And you'll be twice as lucky if they work at zoos, theme parks, bakeries, toy factories, or sporting goods stores.

| Do | Don't |
|---|---|
| . . . be polite and respectful. | . . . pull the fire alarm. |
| . . . address the boss as "Mr." or "Ms." | . . . address the boss as "Scrooge," "Warden," or "Dungeon Master." |
| . . . admire your parent's office. | . . . say, "This is smaller than your last office." |
| . . . be friendly to coworkers. | . . . ask, "Are you that guy who has the same job my mom does but gets paid more?" |
| . . . keep your hands to yourself. | . . . steal office supplies, even if instructed to do so by parent. |
| . . . make the best possible impression. | . . . make photocopies of your butt. |

"Money can't buy happiness." You've heard it a hundred times, and you're gonna hear it hundreds more, because it's what grown-ups say when they don't feel like paying for something you want. This is sneaky and underhanded, but like much of what adults say, it's true . . . partly. The fact is, money does buy happiness—*but only up to a point*.

## The Principle of Diminishing Returns

Economists use this fancy name for a simple principle that any kid understands, especially when it's called by a more descriptive name: "The Principle of Hot Fudge Sundaes." Here's how it works:

As the last of these four pictures shows, it really is possible to get too much of a good thing. That's The Principle of Diminishing Returns in a nutshell. But adults have a hard time applying it to money. That's why they knock themselves out trying to make so darned much of it—they remember how happy they felt earning their first dollar (babysitting or mowing lawns or whatever), so they figure that earning a million dollars will make them a million times as happy, right?

Wrong. It might not even make them *ten* times as happy. Because earning a million bucks can be a lot of trouble. They might end up having to work really hard and ignore their families, make enemies, and worry constantly about losing all the money. They might even be *less* happy than they were before the million!

## Tactic #23:
## Keeping Score in the Game of Life

One way to avoid getting all bent out of shape about money is to think of it as points in a game. Only you don't win it by earning more points than somebody else, you win it by always having enough points to buy yourself something fun (like a hot fudge sundae) once in a while.

Mr. Micawber, a character in Charles Dickens's classic book *David Copperfield*, summed the whole subject up more or less like this: "Annual income $25,000, annual expenditures $25,100, result misery. Annual income $25,000, annual expenditures $24,900, result happiness." This concept is so simple, even an adult should be able to understand it.

Grown-ups experience sports in two ways: as participants (playing) or as spectators (yelling). In both cases the sporting event, or "game," causes the grown-up to undergo a mysterious transformation, often into something nearly unrecognizable.

- **Playing.** Relaxed, responsible, reasonable, rational—these words describe most adults as they calmly go about their daily routine. But stick a golf club, tennis racket, or even Ping-Pong paddle in their hand, and what do you get? A bawling, flailing two-year-old, convinced that the future of the human race depends on his ability to propel some kind of object toward some kind of target harder, faster, or more accurately than another adult can.

- **Watching.** Spectator sports have an even weirder effect—especially when you consider that the spectator rarely has anything in common with the team he's rooting for but the color of the cap, jersey, or jacket that he wears on game days. The power of televised sports to reduce a full-grown adult to the mental state of a Tasmanian devil is beyond the scope of this book, and is better left to psychiatrists. In the meantime, here's a typical story.

## The Story of Dan

True story: Dan, 34, of Rancho Cucamonga, California, is a friendly, responsible guy. But every time (his) beloved University of Michigan plays Ohio State in football, he loses his voice for three days from *screaming at the TV* screen. You see, Dan actually thinks that his screaming *helps*—that without it, the Wolverines would have no clue what to do out there on the field. That's right, he believes that his shrill cries will travel into his TV, through outer space, and all the way to the stadium, where the quarterback will hear him shouting and say, "Hey, guys, I think Dan really wants us to make this first down! I was planning to throw an interception, but I just changed my mind . . . *whaddaya say we win this one for the Danner?*"

## Tactic #24:
## How to Play Defense Against an Offensive Grown-Up

1. Don't ever stand between an adult and a TV showing a sporting event, except during the ads. (And during the Super Bowl, not during the ads, either.)

2. Never say out loud the results or score of a game sooner than two days after it was played—an adult may have TiVoed it.

3. Never compete against a grown-up in any sport where you have a good chance of winning—their egos can't handle the loss. The one exception is where (a.) the grown-up insists, and (b.) you're positive that you have the edge. Then bet on the contest, and bet big. You'll be doing the grown-up a favor by teaching them to pick on somebody their own size next time.

# 26
# Toys
## Like Yours, Only Way More Expensive

It's said that "the main difference between men and boys is the price of their toys." And for adults who can't stop shopping, the Big Three are **Electronics, Cars,** and **Real Estate:**

1. **Electronics.** More and more, adults are filling their homes and offices with enough electronic and computing power to launch a satellite. Only what they *actually* use it for is keeping an address book, trying and failing to figure out their taxes, playing solitaire, and spending hours with online tech support, hoping to make sense of it all.

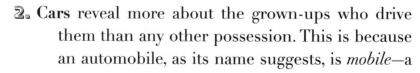

2. **Cars** reveal more about the grown-ups who drive them than any other possession. This is because an automobile, as its name suggests, is *mobile*—a

kind of rolling billboard that shouts to the world, "I may be bald, but my convertible proves that I'm still young and carefree" or "My three-quarter-ton pickup shows I'm ready to crush your lifeless corpse into the pavement" or "As the driver of a fuel-efficient hybrid, I'm obviously kind and caring, so don't complain if I steal your parking space."

If houses could be driven down the street, they would have lots of polished grillwork around the front door, spinning chrome window frames, and license plate holders that read, "My other house is a mansion." Which brings us to . . .

3. **Real Estate**, the most costly item by far in the adult toy box. There comes a moment in every adult's

life when they awaken with a burning desire to own dirt, and lots of it. Especially if there's a house sitting on the dirt. Then they decorate those houses. Then they redecorate. Then they re-redecorate. Then one day they realize they have too much stuff for the house, so they get *more* dirt, with a bigger house on it, which leads to more stuff, and so on.

# A Brief History of Property

The concept of "ownership" goes back a looooooooooong way—precisely, to a damp Thursday afternoon during the late caveman period, when a Neanderthal named Tony was trying to get rid of another guy named Phil who had overstayed his welcome in Tony's cave and kept telling dinosaur jokes.

Phil went back to his cave to take an aspirin and then returned in a half hour with several of his largest friends to teach Tony a lesson, but Tony had in the meantime rounded up a few of *his* friends, and the two groups fought. Phil's group won, and Tony had to hand over the keys to the cave.

From that day to this, grown-ups have been fussing and fighting over who owns what, pausing only to remind their children, "Remember to share, kids."

# 27
# LOVE
## Is It as Icky as It Seems?

In a word, yes. No, it's even worse.

Traditional, full-blown, romantic love between two adults, as celebrated in songs, stories, and big-budget Hollywood movies, is every bit as disgusting to behold as it sounds. It may include one or more of the following:

- Hand-holding
- Hugging
- Kissing
- Staring deep into each other's eyes
- Talking for hours about nothing at all
- Use of the terms "dear," "darling," "baby," "honey," "sweetums," and "sugar lips"
- Mutual grooming
- Feeding each other little tastes of food in restaurants

Even more sickeningly, your own parents (or *grandparents*!) may sometimes carry on like this, in broad daylight.

Ever wonder how such ancient organisms can go on cuddling year after year, no matter how much hair they've lost or weight they've gained since they were high school sweethearts? The secret is that the aging process happens *extre-e-e-mely slo-o-o-wly*. Couples take so long to decay (like plutonium) that neither one notices what's happening. And to make things even easier, their eyesight fails at about the same rate—as far as they can tell, the face looking back at them across the dinner table stays pretty much the same, year in and year out. (You can experience this phenomenon yourself the next time you go to a zoo. If you squint your eyes hard enough while staring at a rhinoceros, it will look exactly like a puppy.)

## ♥ ♥ Love Is Gonna Getcha ♥ ♥

The fact is, nothing can be done about love. It is, as they say, here to stay. And it's a good thing, too, because without love the human race wouldn't exist from generation to generation, and then who would buy books like this one?

And the most bizarre, impossible-to-believe part of it all is, all of this craziness will happen to *you*, and *you will like it*. Yes, you really and truly will!

Most people work up to the Big L in a series of small steps, like the onset of a chronic and incurable disease, until you finally reach the One Great Love of Your Life. This handy chart will help you recognize the steps:

## What You Feel and What You Feel That Way About

♥ ♥ ♥

**The One Great Love of Your Life** ♥

**Crush** ↗ Teacher, classmates, pop stars

**Passion** ↗ Video games, movies

**Devotion** ↗ Sports teams

**Fondness** ↗ Friends

**Close bond** ↗ Dogs/cats

**Tolerance** ↗ Brothers/sisters

**Affection** ↗ Parents

**Enjoyment** ↗ Ice cream, oatmeal

**Satisfaction** Full stomach, clean diaper

# The Recipe for Love

## Ingredients

- **You**

- **Object of affection**

- **2 movie tickets**

- **1 park bench**

- **1 box of chocolates, assorted**

- **1 beach, long**

- **1 moon, full**

## Instructions

- **Warm oven** to temperature of cat asleep in your lap
- **Add to bowl:** excitement of first successful bike ride without training wheels
- **Dust with:** first snowfall of winter
- **Sprinkle with:** warm summer rain
- **Garnish with:** chills, fever, feeling of being balanced on the back legs of a chair
- **Bake until done.** You'll know you're in love when (a.) you're convinced that no one in history has ever experienced this totally awesome state except you; and (b.) you feel like hurling

The One Great Love of Your Life will rapidly be followed by the Second Great Love of Your Life, the Third, and possibly the First again.

During all of this uproar your heart will be broken, patched up, broken again, and generally treated like a torn old dishrag that keeps being buried and dug up by a series of increasingly ferocious dogs.

Actually, the best part of finding the Great Love of Your Life is that you'll get to keep all the advantages of a best friend (which you may already have), *plus* numerous benefits that are a bit too racy for this book.

And that's all that needs to be said at present. For the rest, just stick around for several years, and let nature take its course. It's well worth the wait.

# 28
## ADULT IDENTIFICATION GUIDE
### How to Tell the Bakers from the Bankers

By now it should be apparent that adults come in a vast variety of shapes, sizes, and functions . . . most of them annoying. It would be impossible to fully describe every grown-up—Lady Gaga alone would take at least thirty pages—but here's a list of some of the most common types that you're likely to encounter.

You might even want to make a hobby of it. Capturing specimens of grown-ups with a net and pinning them to a board like butterflies is illegal (not to mention impractical), but you can always start your own "virtual adult collection." You will need:

- A pair of **binoculars**, for discreet observation;
- A **notebook**, in which to describe and classify their behavior;
- An inexpensive **camera**, to document sightings (avoid using a flash, as adults are easily startled);
- **Snacks** and **treats**, for luring specimens into close range (always keep a few energy bars, smoked almonds, and chocolates handy; if these don't work, try Starbucks gift cards). And finally,

◉ An **"Adult call."** This is a small recording device equipped with a speaker that broadcasts messages irresistible to adults, such as "Great outfit," "50 percent off!" and "Your table is ready."

Happy hunting!

## Actor

**Other Names:** Thespian, Player, Prima Donna

**Latin Name:** *Celebrati Starlicius*

**Natural Habitat:** Stage, screen, unemployment line, in front of a mirror

**Identifying Characteristics:** Ego, vanity, fabulousness. In France they call an actor a *m'as-tu-vu* ("have you seen me?"). Actors feel they *must* be seen, or they stop existing. Before they get famous, they'll beg you to come to every weird little play they appear in. (After they get famous, they won't return your calls, unless they want to borrow money.) Yet despite all this, they're almost impossible to dislike, maybe because they're so good at acting likable.

**Pros:** Ability to make us glow in the reflected light of their dazzling stardom

**Cons:** Awards shows

**What Not to Say to One:** "Hey, aren't you [name of different actor]?"

# Athlete

**Other Names:** Competitor, Sportsman, Shortstop

**Latin Name:** *Biggus Strongus Fastus*

**Natural Habitat:** Courts, fields, pools, boxing rings, ski slopes (Not bowling alleys. Bowling is not a sport but an excuse to wear funny shirts, crack jokes, drink beer, and bond.)

**Identifying Characteristics:** Muscle tone, motivation, overuse of the word "motivation."

Athletes tend to see the entire world in terms of competition. To them an election is a Race, a long day at the office is a Marathon, and everyone they meet is either a Winner or a Loser. They like to say, "It's not whether you win or lose, it's how you play the game," but deep down inside they believe that life is, in fact, about whether you win or lose.

**Pros:** Handy to have on your side in a fight, especially boxers, wrestlers, and fencers

**Cons:** Tendency to speak in sports clichés, narrow range of interests, B.O.

**What Not to Say to One:** "*I can do that.*" (They might make you prove it.)

# Dentist

**Other Names:** Orthodontist, Drill Jockey, Smile Mechanic, Tooth Burglar

**Latin Name:** Dentalis Openwidius

**Natural Habitat:** Your gaping mouth, ADA conventions, yacht

**Identifying Characteristics:** Steady hands; ability to carry on one-sided conversations; fresh, minty smell.

Dentists occupy an uncomfortable rung on the ladder of health care providers: one rung below doctors. That's because doctors are well-known for their ability to cure diseases, save lives, and reattach severed legs, but dentists, no matter how skilled, will always be associated with the words "pain," "drill," and "spit sink."

But dentists do have one important advantage. If a doctor starts to tell a patient an old joke, the patient can say, "Sorry, I've heard it." If a dentist does, all the patient can say is "Aaaghrghhughlllugglugluigishhhh."

**Pros:** Skill, competence, cleanliness

**Cons:** Not entirely honest when they say "This won't hurt a bit"

**What Not to Say to One:** "Heard any good ones lately?"

# Doctor

**Other Names:** Physician, MD, Sawbones, Croaker

**Latin Name:** *Dissectus Medicali*

**Natural Habitat:** Office, operating room, golf course

**Identifying Characteristics:** White coat or green scrubs, stethoscope, air of superiority. It's hard to believe, but they *don't* want to hurt you—even though they've got about a zillion ways to do so. In fact the opposite is true: if they make you worse instead of better, you'll find another doctor; if they injure you, you'll sue them (see "Types of Adults: Lawyer"); and if they kill you, they'll have to replace you with another patient. This leaves them with healing as their only remaining course of action.

**Pros:** Ability to save your life

**Cons:** Ability to end your life

**What Not to Say to One:** "I don't have insurance."

# Lawyer

**Other Names:** Attorney, Counselor, Ambulance-Chaser, Mouth-piece (Note: only the first two are considered flattering)

**Latin Name:** *Juris Doctor*, which means "teacher of law." That's right, it's not enough for them to know the law—they're gonna teach it to you.

**Natural Habitat:** Courtroom, boardroom, corner office, Congress

**Identifying Characteristics:** Intelligence, mastery of difficult language, overwhelming confidence (especially those who went to Harvard).

Lawyers come in two flavors, "civil" and "criminal." *Civil* lawyers are all about helping their clients (customers) get and keep money and property, which is a big job, because everybody wants more money and property. *Criminal* lawyers are all about keeping their clients from paying fines or going to jail. Civil lawyers usually make more money, which is the origin of the saying "Crime doesn't pay."

**Pros:** Well-spoken, well-schooled, well-dressed

**Cons:** The best ones charge $1,000 an hour

**What Not to Say to One:** "A thousand bucks an hour? For what?" Because they'll spend an hour explaining why they charge so much, and now you're out another grand.

# Millionaire

**Other Names:** Person of Means, VIP, High Roller, Mr. Moneybags

**Latin Name:** *Lifestylus Deluxo*

**Natural Habitat:** Limousines, country clubs, penthouse apartments, private jets, head of list, top of heap

**Identifying Characteristics:** Vast piles of dough that they like to throw around—in your direction, if you're lucky.

Making friends among the superrich is well worth the effort, as it lets you experience luxury without having to put in the hard work of earning it yourself.

There's truth in the saying "It's lonely at the top." Don't let them be lonely! Wealth, like food and drink, is most enjoyable when shared— especially when it's shared with you.

**Pros:** Front-row seats, skyboxes, best tables at restaurants

**Cons:** Egomania, eccentricity, arrogance, tendency to bully others

**What Not to Say to One:** Any of the "cons." You do, after all, want to be asked back.

# Musician

**Other Names:** Instrumentalist, Virtuoso, Performer

**Latin Name:** *Maestro Diva Musicali*

**Natural Habitat:** Coffee shop (waiting tables for low wages or playing for even lower wages); college dorm stairwell (for the echo-chamber effect); concert stage (but only if everything goes *exactly* right in their careers)

**Identifying Characteristics:** Creative spirit, sensitive eyes, wide range of complaints.

Musicians possess the amazing talent to create angelic sounds that speak directly to our souls and stir us to the very core of our being. Also, they usually work cheap—or, if there's food to be had, for free.

**Pros:** Gushing with music at all times

**Cons:** Gushing with music at all times

**What Not to Say to One:** "Will you play solo . . . *so low* that I can't hear you?" They have heard this one many times, and just may respond with a trombone slide to your nose.

# Police Officer

**Other Names:** Cop, John Law, Flatfoot, The Fuzz, The Man

**Latin Name:** *Crimus Interruptus*

**Natural Habitat:** Police stations, the beat, crime scenes, doughnut shops

**Identifying Characteristics:** Uniform, badge, machismo. Often heard speaking in a secret code only understood by other officers and cop show fanatics. "Officer 2817, this is Officer 6925. I've got a 505 engaged in a 586E with possible 915. I'll 961 him and 10-17 before I Code 7." (Translation: "Bob, it's Debbie. I've got a reckless driver who might also be a litterbug blocking a driveway. I'll make a report and stop by the station before lunch.")

Police officers have a lot of power, so they can be forgiven if they swagger a little. And considering the amount of soul-crushing boredom they face each day, interrupted by explosions of violence and danger—all on a salary not much higher than a cashier's—they certainly deserve our respect. Just the same, what's with all the mustaches?

**Pros:** Serving, protecting, keeping the peace

**Cons:** Can turn you into a con

**What Not to Say to One:** "I bet that's not a real gun."

# Writer

**Other Names:** Author, Journalist, Scribbler, Pencil-Pusher, Ink-Stained Wretch

**Latin Name:** *Blabbermouthus Literati*

**Natural Habitat:** Library, vegetable garden, hardware store, Laundromat—anyplace but where they should be, which is chained to a desk, slamming down the sentences

**Identifying Characteristics:** Large vocabulary, deep (though not always broad) knowledge of literature, history, and public affairs. A writer can give you a detailed outline of every one of Shakespeare's plays, yet be totally unaware that he hasn't washed his hair in three weeks and tiny critters are now crawling around on his scalp.

Almost every kid dreams at some point of becoming a writer, and some actually manage to pull it off. There's an old saying that writing can't be taught, but it can be learned. So you may have a bright career as an author ahead of you—writing draft after draft of the same book, waiting for royalty checks, and praying each night for success for yourself and failure for your other author friends.

**Pros:** Imaginative, thoughtful, well-read

**Cons:** Jumpy, irritable, convinced that another writer stole the plot of their new novel

**What Not to Say to One:** "I just signed a three-book deal. How's it going with you?"

FAQs:
Wild

**Q:** Why do grown-ups keep how much money they earn a secret?

**A:** Because they have nothing to gain by telling. If it isn't much, they're ashamed; if it's a lot, they're afraid that either (a.) another grown-up will steal it, or (b.) their brother-in-law will borrow it and never pay it back, which amounts to the same thing.

☺ ☺ ☺

**Q:** Why do adults wear watches?

**A:** They say it's so that they won't be late for appointments, but it's really so they can keep glancing at them in order to look busy and important when they're actually goofing off.

☺ ☺ ☺

**Q:** Why do they talk down to us?

**A:** To put off as long as possible the unpleasant truth that you're rapidly catching up with them mentally, and will soon blow past them and leave them in the dust, which you're going to do anyway, whether they like it or not.

The world would be a much better place if grown-ups spoke to kids the same way they speak to each other. If they use a word you don't know, stop them and ask what it means. If they don't know, accuse them of being a phony. (A perfect example is the word "paradigm." Nobody knows what "paradigm" means.)

❂ ❂ ❂

**Q:** Why don't they watch Saturday morning cartoons?

**A:** They do—they just watch them at different times, in slightly different forms. Movies and television shows are really nothing but Saturday morning cartoons dressed up in a suit and tie. In fact, three of the last five Oscar winners were based on old episodes of *SpongeBob SquarePants*.

❂ ❂ ❂

**Q:** Are adults afraid?

**A:** Yes, but not as afraid as kids are. They *worry* more, but they spend much less time being actually terrified. In fact, one huge benefit of growing up is that you outgrow most of your irrational fears—many eight-year-olds are afraid of thunderstorms or closet monsters, but few thirty-eight-year-olds are. (Although some thirty-eight-year-olds dream that they're being chased by the Boogie Man.)

# PART 5:
# THREE UNIVERSAL TRUTHS

**B**y this point you've probably had about enough of theories, and can't wait to explode into the real world and actually put these ideas into practice. But there are still three more nuggets of truth to go, and they are very valuable nuggets indeed. In fact, one reason they're so powerful is that they can help you get through both childhood *and* adulthood.

Ready? Here they are:

# Truth #1
## Clean Up as You Go Along

It's tempting to toss this one in the garbage along with the rest of the Annoying Adult Advice, such as "slow and steady wins the race" (have adults never seen an Olympic sprinter?) and "if you don't have something nice to say, don't say anything" (what if you have to tell someone they're on fire?).

"Clean up as you go along" may sound like a cruel rule designed to turn happy children into miserable slaves, but it's really an incredibly valuable principle. That's because although it sounds like it would create more work for you, it actually creates *less*—by getting all the crud out of your own way, you can finish up whatever job you're doing faster and easier, resulting in more time to do actual fun stuff, such as making prank phone calls.

"Clean up as you go along." The

bigger the stakes, the better it works. Yet very few adults ever master it, which explains filthy garages, overstuffed attics, most bankruptcies, and the Korean War, which actually grew from a misunderstanding involving a peanut butter sandwich. (Okay, that's not literally true, but it's *figuratively* true.)

To illustrate the rule's value, here's what happens if you break it:

STEP 1: Let's say you've hurt a classmate's feelings by pointing out in front of everybody that her nose is the size of Panama. You know you did a Bad Thing, and you want to say you're sorry. But apologizing is no fun, so—

STEP 2: —you put it off till after the weekend. Meanwhile Panama-nose is stewing like a pot of bubbling chemical waste, and she and her friends hatch a fiendish way to get even with you. And on Monday—

STEP 3: —they execute a brilliant scheme to de-pants you during a nature hike. By this time you can apologize all you want, but it's too late, because there you are with your jeans around your ankles and mosquitoes feasting on your pudgy legs, and everybody will be laughing too hard to hear what you're saying, anyway.

Now, if you'd only made the effort to say you were sorry when you had the chance, this revolting situation could have been avoided. You and El Schnozzo may even have become friends, teaming up to de-pants somebody else.

# TRUTH # 2:
## Use the Right Tool for the Job

Everyone violates this one now and then, including, probably, surgeons. ("What, we don't have any scalpels? That's okay, I can saw off this appendix with my car keys.") That's because it's so easy to get caught up in what we're doing that we cheat and take a shortcut, then regret it later. Again, here's an illustration, in four painful steps:

STEP 1: Suppose you need to remove the front wheel of your mountain bike. A mechanic would use a crescent wrench, but that's because mechanics *have* crescent wrenches. All you've got is a cheap adjustable wrench, only it isn't in the toolbox where it should be, it's in the basement. And you don't want to go *all the way downstairs* for it, so instead—

STEP 2: —you use a pair of greasy pliers. Only the pliers slip off the nut and you bust your knuckles against the spokes, and now you're bleeding. You'd normally put a Band-Aid on a scrape like this, but they're *all the way in the upstairs bathroom*, so instead—

**STEP 3:** —you wrap an old rag around your fingers— the same rag you used yesterday to throw away a dead rat. Now you're well on your way to having rabies. But you've got a more important task on your mind: *getting that wheel off.* You really should drop the bike project altogether and go wash your hands with hot, soapy water, but that would require you to go *all the way to the kitchen,* so instead—

**STEP 4:** —you spit on your knuckles and wipe them on the grass, which unfortunately is full of stinging nettles. When you're done screaming, you finally give up on the wheel and trudge back into the house, all bloody and oily and in pain and with rabies, and all because you didn't Use the Right Tool for the Job.

Another nice thing about this Universal Adult Truth is that it's so easy to spot violations. So next time you see a grown-up using a butter knife for a screwdriver, or a shoe for a hammer, or a flimsy chair for a stepladder, come right out with it: "Use the right tool for the job!" Then if they ignore your advice and screw everything up, you'll be entitled to utter the four sweetest words in the English language: "I told you so."

# TRUTH # 3:

## A Thing Is Not Necessarily True Just Because an Adult Said It

Okay, *most* of what they say is true . . . but not everything. And it's up to *you* to separate fact from fiction, exaggeration, and just plain nonsense.

If an adult says something that isn't true, it's generally for one of the following three reasons:

1. **They're lying.** Yep, just like kids. Sometimes they do it to be kind ("What a beautiful dress, Aunt Jennifer!"), sometimes to cover their own butts ("Honest, my alarm didn't go off this morning!"), and sometimes because they're just afraid to tell the truth ("I didn't see the stop sign, officer!").

   Grown-ups are always getting better and better at lying, which means *you* need to get better and better at seeing through the lies. If you do, you win and they lose, because you won't buy what they're selling. If you don't, then they win and *you* lose, because they've made you look like a chump. Pay attention, and you can beat them at their own game.

**2: They're crazy.** Not completely crazy, and not crazy all the time. But grown-ups definitely have their moments.

Here's an example. Most tall buildings in America don't have a thirteenth floor. They actually do, of course (it's the one sitting directly on top of the twelfth floor, duh), but if you examine the building directory or the numbers on the elevator buttons, there's no "13." It skips straight to "14." That's because enough people suffer from triskaidekaphobia (a superstitious fear of the number thirteen) that the sign makers and elevator-button labelers decided it's easier just to omit that number than to go out and cure all those nutty people.

And it doesn't end there. Continental Airlines—a real airline, owned and run by real adults—*has no thirteenth row in its planes*.

If a grown-up in your life is driving you crazy with their craziness (for example, not letting you go outside until they check your horoscope), call them on it. But you won't get anywhere by telling them they're acting crazy—tell them they're acting *childish*. You're much more likely to get results.

**3: They hate to admit they're wrong.** Grown-ups have

a very, very hard time admitting to each other that they've messed up, let alone admitting it to a kid. They're afraid it'll weaken their authority—if they confess that it was a mistake to blow two thousand bucks on lottery tickets or get a skull tattooed on their arm when they were in their twenties, then what right do they have to boss *you* around?

Kids don't like to admit mistakes either, but they have an easier time of it because, hey, they're only kids. (There's even a whole list of sayings that apply to this situation: "Boys will be boys," "She's just going through a phase," "It's an awkward stage.")

But once people get a bit older, they start expecting each other (and themselves) to do everything *right* all the time—which is, of course, impossible. Adults are constantly screwing up (the Spanish Inquisition, mullet haircuts, the Vietnam War, slavery, disco, etc.), so they shouldn't be embarrassed to admit the mistake, learn a lesson, and move on. The generation that's currently in charge hasn't figured this out yet, but maybe yours will.

# CONCLUSION
## Growing Up Without Growing Old

Yes, one day you will—sure as gravity, taxes, and bad movie sequels—become a grown-up yourself. And it's understandable to fear that reaching adulthood will mean trading in all the fun stuff *you* do for all the dull stuff *they* do.

Guess what: it won't! That's because (as mentioned back in the Preface), the way you live your life as a kid may be dictated by grown-ups, but the way you'll live your life as an adult is *totally up to you!*

Sure, after age twenty-one or so you'll have to start paying your own way and perform a lot of drudgery (you won't *believe* the number of forms you'll be required to fill out) but generally speaking, adulthood doesn't really have to be all that different from childhood, if you don't want it to be. Instead of putting away childish things, no one can stop you from *hanging on to* childish things (or at least the best ones, such as a sense of wonder and an open mind) and adding a bunch of great *new* stuff, such as power, intelligence, wisdom, judgment . . . in a word, maturity.

Some of today's adults have taken this "freedom road," too, occasionally with freakish results (bad boy Mick Jagger is almost seventy, and has been demanding satisfaction for five decades). But overall it's probably a good thing. Because if *you* hit middle age and still want to chew watermelon gum and blow bubbles as big as your head, or make a spectacle of yourself on the dance floor at your daughter's bat mitzvah or be seen riding a bike in those gross tight, black shorts, well . . . what's the harm? The worst that can happen is that you'll embarrass your kids, which is only fair—look at the way your parents embarrassed you.

Turning into an adult means lots of things. If you do it right, it means staying up late yet wanting to get up early; making friends that won't necessarily leave for another town at the end of the school year; and—quite possibly—making one superawesome friend that will never leave, period. To put it simply, it means enjoying things that you can't enjoy now, and no longer being scared of stuff that scares you now.

But perhaps most of all, being a grown-up means thinking for yourself. If you don't, another adult will be all too happy to do it for you—in which case, you'll just be a kid in a grown-up's body. How sad is that?

Come to think of it, you don't even have to wait to grow up to think for yourself. You can do it right now.

**Monte Montgomery** is the coauthor of *Hubert Invents the Wheel*. His work has also been produced on stage, screen, and television. The son of a dancer and a scientist, Monte has been a waiter, truck driver, legal secretary, songwriter, playwright, novelist, public health consultant, jazz pianist, and movie director. He and his wife, Claire, live in Washington DC, where they're still trying to figure out what to be when (and if) they grow up.

www.claireandmonte.com

**Patricia Storms** has illustrated several children's books, editorial cartoons, and humor gift books. She lives and creates in Toronto, Ontario, with her husband, Guy, and two fat cats in a 93-year-old house that's full to the brim with books.

www.patriciastorms.com